Gretchen Bitterlin
Dennis Johnson
Donna Price
Sylvia Ramirez
K. Lynn Savage, Series Editor

Ventures 3
WORKBOOK

with Ingrid Wisniewska

CAMBRIDGE
UNIVERSITY PRESS

CAMBRIDGE UNIVERSITY PRESS
Cambridge, New York, Melbourne, Madrid, Cape Town, Singapore,
São Paulo, Delhi, Dubai, Tokyo, Mexico City

Cambridge University Press
32 Avenue of the Americas, New York, NY 10013–2473, USA

www.cambridge.org
Information on this title: www.cambridge.org/9780521679602

First published 2008
10th printing 2011

Printed in the United States of America

A catalog record for this publication is available from the British Library.

ISBN 978-0-521-60099-6 pack consisting of Student's Book and Audio CD
ISBN 978-0-521-67960-2 Workbook
ISBN 978-0-521-6981-7 pack consisting of Teacher's Edition and Teacher's Toolkit Audio CD / CD-ROM
ISBN 978-0-521-67730-1 CDs (Audio)
ISBN 978-0-521-67761-8 Cassettes
ISBN 978-0-521-67585-7 Add Ventures

Art direction, book design, photo research, and layout services: Adventure House, NYC

Contents

Unit 1 *Personal information*   2

Unit 2 *At school*   14

Unit 3 *Friends and family*   26

Unit 4 *Health*   38

Unit 5 *Around town*   50

Unit 6 *Time*   62

Unit 7 *Shopping*   74

Unit 8 *Work*   86

Unit 9 *Daily living*   98

Unit 10 *Leisure*   110

Reference charts   122

Answer key   130

Personal information

1 Read the story. Circle the answers.

Juliana

Anika

Juliana and Anika are friends. Juliana is quiet and shy. She dislikes going to dance clubs or other noisy places. She often writes e-mails to her friends, but she doesn't like meeting new people. She likes being alone or meeting with just one or two friends. On the weekend, she likes staying home. She loves reading and watching movies. Last weekend, she read two books and watched three movies.

Anika is very different from Juliana. She is friendly and outgoing. She dislikes being alone at home. She loves meeting new people and talking on her cell phone. On the weekend, she enjoys dancing and going to parties with a group of her friends. Last night, they went to a dance club and danced until 3:00 in the morning.

1. Juliana dislikes _____ .
   a. going out
   b. reading books
   c. watching movies

2. Juliana likes _____ .
   a. meeting people
   b. talking
   c. staying home

3. Juliana isn't _____ .
   a. quiet
   b. outgoing
   c. shy

4. Anika dislikes _____ .
   a. dancing
   b. going to parties
   c. staying home

5. Anika likes _____ .
   a. making friends
   b. staying home
   c. being alone

6. Anika isn't _____ .
   a. outgoing
   b. friendly
   c. shy

Check your answers. See page 130.

2 Complete the sentences. Use the information in Exercise 1.

alone	dislikes	going out	party animal
dance club	enjoys	outgoing	shy

1. Juliana is not a _____ *party animal* _____ .

2. Anika is an _____ person.

3. Juliana _____ meeting with only one or two people at a time.

4. Anika likes _____ with her friends.

5. Juliana _____ going to parties.

6. Anika was at the _____ until 3:00 a.m.

7. Juliana is quiet and _____ .

8. Anika doesn't like being _____ .

3 Circle the correct word.

1. Pietro is quiet. He **enjoys** / (**dislikes**) talking.

2. Salma is outgoing. She **enjoys** / **dislikes** meeting new people.

3. Chen is friendly. He **enjoys** / **dislikes** talking to other people.

4. Naomi is shy. She **enjoys** / **dislikes** meeting new people.

5. Enrico is not a party animal. He **enjoys** / **dislikes** going out.

6. Max is a party animal. He **enjoys** / **dislikes** going out.

4 Write the opposites.

different	dislike	outgoing	quiet	stay home

1. shy: _____ *outgoing* _____

2. noisy: _____

3. go out: _____

4. same: _____

5. like: _____

Check your answers. See page 130.

Verbs + gerunds

Study the chart and explanation on page 122.

1 Read the chart. Complete the sentences. Use gerunds.

	Francisco	Erika	Chang
playing soccer	✓✓	✓	✓
doing homework	✓	X	O
getting up early	O	O	XX

Key	✓= likes	✓✓ = loves	X = dislikes	XX = hates	O = doesn't mind

1. Chang hates _____*getting up early*_____ .

2. Erika dislikes _____ .

3. Chang doesn't mind _____ .

4. Francisco loves _____ .

5. Erika and Chang like _____ .

6. Francisco and Erika don't mind _____ .

2 Circle the answers. Use the information in Exercise 1.

1. Does Francisco like doing homework? (Yes, he does.) / No, he doesn't.

2. Does Erika dislike getting up early? Yes, she does. / No, she doesn't.

3. Does Chang dislike doing homework? Yes, he does. / No, he doesn't.

4. Do Erika and Chang like playing soccer? Yes, they do. / No, they don't.

5. Does Chang like getting up early? Yes, he does. / No, he doesn't.

6. Does Francisco mind getting up early? Yes, he does. / No, he doesn't.

Check your answers. See page 130.

3 Complete the sentences. Use gerunds.

| be | do | go out | listen | play | read | surf | work |

Antonio loves __going out__ with his friends. He hates _____
   (1)   (2)
alone. In English class, he likes _____ in small groups. He doesn't
                                        (3)
mind _____ the textbook or _____ to a CD. He dislikes
        (4)   (5)
_____ homework. On the weekend, Antonio and his friends enjoy
   (6)
_____ soccer. They also like _____ the Internet.
   (7)   (8)

4 Complete the sentences. Then write answers. Use the information in Exercise 3.

1. **A** Does Antonio like _____*going out*_____ with his friends?
                                 (go out)

   B *Yes, he does* .

2. **A** Does he hate _____ alone?
                           (be)

   B _____ .

3. **A** Does he mind _____ the textbook?
                           (read)

   B _____ .

4. **A** Does he like _____ homework?
                           (do)

   B _____ .

5 Write *Yes / No* questions. Use gerunds.

1. you / enjoy / go to the beach

   Do you enjoy going to the beach ?

2. you / dislike / stand in line

   _____ ?

3. you / like / play cards

   _____ ?

4. you / mind / take out the garbage

   _____ ?

Check your answers. See page 130.

Lesson C Comparisons

Study the explanation on page 128.

1 Read the paragraph. Complete the chart.

> Angelina likes cooking more than watching movies. She likes reading less than watching movies. She enjoys dancing more than cooking, but she likes dancing less than socializing with her friends. She likes socializing as much as playing sports.

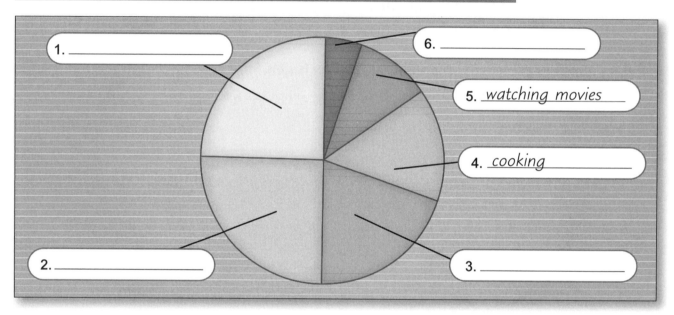

1. _____

6. _____

5. *watching movies*

4. *cooking*

2. _____

3. _____

2 Write sentences about Angelina.

1. cooking / watching movies (less than)

   Angelina likes watching movies less than cooking.

2. watching movies / reading (more than)

   _____

3. dancing / cooking (less than)

   _____

4. dancing / socializing (more than)

   _____

5. playing sports / socializing (as much as)

   _____

Check your answers. See page 130.

3 Look at the pictures. Complete the sentences about the people in the pictures. Use *more than*.

playing an instrument / painting

driving a car / riding a bicycle

reading / washing the dishes

shopping / going to the movies

1. Ling likes *painting more than playing an instrument* .

2. Frank enjoys _____ .

3. Suzanna enjoys _____ .

4. Annie and Steve like _____ .

4 Look at the pictures in Exercise 3. Add the missing word in each sentence.

1. Annie and Steve like shopping less ∧ watching movies. (than)
                           than

2. Ling likes playing an instrument than painting. (less)

3. Suzanna enjoys washing the dishes less reading. (than)

4. Frank enjoys driving a car than riding a bicycle. (less)

Check your answers. See page 130.

Lesson D Reading

1 Before you read, look at the pictures. Predict the job that each ad will describe.

Are you creative? Do you like imagining things? Do you love making things? Do you enjoy thinking of new ideas? We are looking for creative people to join our team of architects. Help us design exciting new homes. Your future is with us!

Job: _____architect_____

Are you intellectual? Do you enjoy solving difficult problems? Do you like working alone more than working in a group? Yes? Then you are the right person for us! We need computer programmers to help create new computers for the future.

Job: _____

Are you friendly and outgoing? Do you like talking with people and helping others? Do you enjoy meeting people and finding out about them? If your answer is yes, then teaching is the job for you. Come and join our friendly team of teachers. Apply today!

Job: _____

2 Read the ads in Exercise 1. Write the best job for each person.

1. Phil is creative. _____architect_____

2. Beverley is intellectual. _____

3. Sarah is outgoing. _____

4. Michael likes working alone. _____

5. Elena enjoys meeting new people. _____

6. Julio loves imagining new ideas. _____

Check your answers. See page 130.

8 Unit 1

3 Match the jobs with the activities. Use the information from the ads in Exercise 1.

| design new things | help students | like learning about other people |
| find answers to problems | imagine new ideas | like working alone |

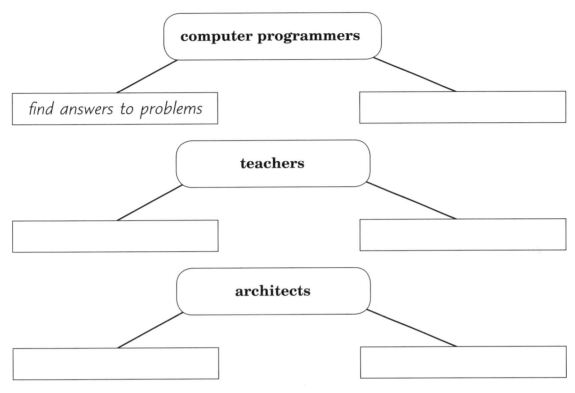

computer programmers

find answers to problems

teachers

architects

4 Complete the sentences.

| artist | creative | friendly | intellectual | outgoing | personality | type |

1. Your ___*personality*___ is the way you think, feel, and act.

2. Su Lin likes thinking and finding answers. She is _____ .

3. Osman enjoys making things. He is _____ .

4. Jenny loves painting and drawing. She wants to be an _____ .

5. Ann enjoys meeting people. She is _____ .

6. Jim's personality _____ is intellectual.

7. Albert likes talking to people and socializing. He's very _____ .

Check your answers. See page 130.

1 Complete the chart.

architect	drawing	helpful	quiet	surfing the Internet
creative	finding answers	helping people	scientist	talking
designer	friendly	outgoing	social worker	teacher

Jobs	Personality adjectives	Activities
architect		

2 Read the paragraph. Complete the chart.

My friend Peter Jones is a social worker at the community center in our town. He is the winner of our town's "Employee of the Month" award. Peter is very friendly and outgoing. He enjoys meeting and helping people who come to the community center. He is also very hardworking. I think Peter has the right job for his personality type.

TOWN EMPLOYEE
OF THE MONTH
AWARD

Name: _Peter Jones_

Job: _____

Place of work: _____

Personality: _____

Likes: _____

Check your answers. See page 130.

3 Read the chart. Complete the sentences.

Name:	Rosa Jamulka
Job:	computer programmer
Place of work:	home
Personality:	quiet and intellectual, careful and hardworking
Likes:	surfing the Internet, finding answers to problems

Rosa Jamulka has the right job for her personality. She's a

computer programmer . She works at home. Rosa is a very quiet and
      1

_____ person. She is also careful and _____ .
      2   3

She loves surfing the Internet, and she enjoys _____ to
                                                      4

problems. Computer programming fits her personality.

4 Read the profile. Write a paragraph about Romano's job and personality type.

My Photo

Romano Pereira's Blog Profile
Age: 33
Gender: male
Job: architect at New Designs Company
Place of work: Raleigh, North Carolina

About me
• creative and helpful
• enjoy drawing
• like imagining things that are new and different

Romano Pereira's job fits his personality. _____

_____

_____

_____

_____

Check your answers. See page 130.

1 Read the questions. Look at the ads. Circle the answers.

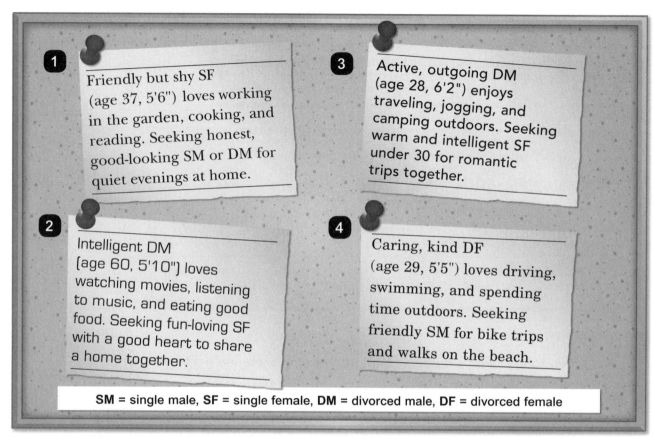

1 Friendly but shy SF (age 37, 5'6") loves working in the garden, cooking, and reading. Seeking honest, good-looking SM or DM for quiet evenings at home.

2 Intelligent DM (age 60, 5'10") loves watching movies, listening to music, and eating good food. Seeking fun-loving SF with a good heart to share a home together.

3 Active, outgoing DM (age 28, 6'2") enjoys traveling, jogging, and camping outdoors. Seeking warm and intelligent SF under 30 for romantic trips together.

4 Caring, kind DF (age 29, 5'5") loves driving, swimming, and spending time outdoors. Seeking friendly SM for bike trips and walks on the beach.

SM = single male, **SF** = single female, **DM** = divorced male, **DF** = divorced female

1. The older man enjoys _____ .
   a. traveling
   b. camping
   c. watching movies
   d. going to the beach

2. The younger woman enjoys _____ .
   a. swimming
   b. gardening
   c. cooking
   d. staying home

3. What word does NOT describe
   the younger man?
   a. shy
   b. active
   c. outgoing
   d. divorced

4. Which two people like going out more
   than staying home?
   a. 1 and 2
   b. 2 and 3
   c. 1 and 4
   d. 3 and 4

5. What does the single female enjoy doing?
   a. traveling
   b. swimming
   c. cooking
   d. driving

6. How tall is the single female?
   a. 5 feet 5 inches
   b. 5 feet 6 inches
   c. 5 feet 10 inches
   d. 6 feet 2 inches

Check your answers. See page 131.

2 Complete the chart.

doing crossword puzzles	going to parties	reading books
drawing	painting pictures	socializing
going to dance clubs	playing chess	taking photos

Creative personality	Intellectual personality	Outgoing personality
	doing crossword puzzles	

3 Complete the puzzle.

architect	artist	creative	intellectual	outgoing	quiet	shy

Across

1. An __ paints, draws, dances, or writes.

3. An __ person likes meeting new people.

4. A __ person is good at making things.

7. An __ designs homes.

Down

2. An __ person enjoys thinking and finding answers.

5. A __ person doesn't talk much.

6. A __ person doesn't like meeting new people.

Check your answers. See page 131.

At school

1 Complete the conversation.

Frank

| concentrate |
| discouraged |
| index cards |
| list |
| paper |
| underline |

Victor Hi, Frank how's it going?

Frank Not so good. Can you help me? I have so much homework. I have to

write a ___*paper*___ for Monday and I have a test tomorrow!
                    1

Victor You need to make a _____ of all your homework. Then write
                                    2

the due date of each item on your calendar.

Frank OK, but what about the test?

Victor You should study your textbook and _____ all the main ideas.
                                                3

Write the important words on _____ and study them in your
                                    4

free time. Do you live near a quiet place where you can _____ ?
                                                                    5

Frank Well, there's a library a few blocks away.

Victor Good! You should study and write your paper there. Don't feel

_____ !
        6

2 Circle the answers. Use the information in Exercise 1.

1. Frank needs some _____ .
   a. homework
   b. advice
   c. friends

2. Frank has to _____ .
   a. study less
   b. help Victor
   c. plan his work

3. Victor is _____ .
   a. boring
   b. helpful
   c. discouraged

4. Victor tells Frank how to _____ .
   a. study smarter
   b. study harder
   c. get to the library

Check your answers. See page 131.

3 Match the sentences.

1. Tami can't finish her book. _d_
2. Bernie underlines the main ideas. _____
3. Sue can't remember new words. _____
4. Pam has too much homework. _____
5. Paolo is not happy. _____
6. The book isn't interesting. _____

a. He is an active reader.
b. He is discouraged.
c. It's boring.
d. She needs to concentrate.
e. She needs to make a list of things to do.
f. She needs to write them on index cards.

4 Complete the sentences.

active	concentrate	index cards	to-do list
boring	discouraged	paper	underline

1. I have to make a _____ to-do list _____ of all my homework.

2. I have to finish this _____ by tomorrow morning.

3. It's hard to _____ in this noisy room.

4. I really need to be a more _____ reader.

5. I need to _____ all the main ideas in this article.

6. I will write the most important information on _____ .

7. This TV show is too _____ . I can't watch it.

8. I feel _____ because I never get all of the answers correct.

5 Mark an ✗ next to the bad study habits. Put a ✓ next to the good study habits.

- ☒ doesn't concentrate
- ☐ doesn't study new words
- ☐ is late for class
- ☐ hands in homework late
- ☐ makes a to-do list
- ☐ hands in homework on time
- ☐ forgets homework
- ☐ doesn't study for the test
- ☐ writes new words on index cards
- ☐ underlines the main ideas

Check your answers. See page 131.

At school 15

Present perfect

Study the chart and explanation on page 124. For a list of irregular verbs, turn to page 127.

1 Circle *for* or *since*.

1. I have known Elsa **(for)** / **since** two years.

2. Tina has taught this class **for** / **since** September.

3. Jasmine has worked in the store **for** / **since** last year.

4. We have lived in Miami **for** / **since** six months.

5. Kelly has had her car **for** / **since** 2007.

6. They have been in the library **for** / **since** 4:00 p.m.

7. I have studied computers **for** / **since** two weeks.

8. They have been in our class **for** / **since** Tuesday.

2 Complete the sentences. Use *have* or *has*.

1. How long __*have*__ you had your car?

2. How long _____ I known you?

3. How long _____ they lived in this city?

4. How long _____ she studied Spanish?

5. How long _____ he been in Canada?

6. How long _____ we worked here?

3 Complete the sentences. Use the present perfect.

1. Bianca works in a restaurant. She _____*has worked*_____ there for five years.

2. Federico and Sonya live in Brazil. They _____ there since April.

3 My sister and I study piano. We _____ piano for fifteen years.

4. Mei Lin has a motorcycle. She _____ a motorcycle since 2005.

5 Mrs. Green teaches English. She _____ English for twelve years.

6 Tom is a student. He _____ a student for three months.

Check your answers. See page 131.

4 Complete the sentences. Write the answers.

A (he / be) How long _____*has he been*_____ on the computer?

B For _____*four hours*_____ .

Since _____*3:00 p.m.*_____ .

A (she / know) How long _____ Dave?

B For _____ .

Since _____ .

A (he / live) How long _____ in the U.S.?

B For _____ .

Since _____ .

5 Write questions. Use the present perfect.

1. they / work / in this school

   How long *have they worked in this school* _____ ?

2. she / have / a driver's license

   How long _____ ?

3. he / live / in this apartment

   How long _____ ?

4. you / be / married

   How long _____ ?

Check your answers. See page 131.

Lesson C *Present perfect*

Study the chart and explanation on page 124. For a list of irregular verbs, turn to page 127.

1 Complete the sentences. Use the correct form of the verb.

1. Have you ever _____ *lost* _____ a library book?
(lose)

2. Has your teacher ever _____ your name?
(forget)

3. Have you ever _____ the newspaper online?
(read)

4. Have you ever _____ the bus to school?
(take)

5. Have you ever _____ the best grade in the class?
(get)

2 Read the chart. Complete the sentences and write the answers.

Study skills survey: Do you . . .	Janice	Hiroshi
1. study English online?	yes	no
2. talk to a school counselor?	no	no
3. make a to-do list?	yes	no
4. write new words in a vocabulary notebook?	yes	yes
5. do your homework on the computer?	yes	no

1. **A** ___*Has*___ Janice ever _____*studied*_____ English online?

    B _*Yes, she has*_____ .

2. **A** _____ Janice and Hiroshi ever _____ to a
    school counselor?

    B _____ .

3. **A** _____ Janice ever _____ a to-do list?

    B _____ .

4. **A** _____ Janice and Hiroshi ever _____ new words
    in a vocabulary notebook?

    B _____ .

5. **A** _____ Hiroshi ever _____ his homework on
    the computer?

    B _____ .

Check your answers. See page 131.

3 Complete the sentences. Use *ever*.

1. ___*Have you ever used*___ the computer in the library?
   (you, use)

2. _____ to you after class?
   (your teacher, talk)

3. _____ with you?
   (your friends, study)

4. _____ an e-mail to your teacher?
   (you, write)

5. _____ the main ideas in your textbook?
   (you, underline)

6. _____ all the questions correct on an English test?
   (you, get)

4 Read the conversations. Write sentences about the people in the conversations.

1. **Kate** Have you ever forgotten to study for a test?

   Melissa No, I haven't.

   Kate Have you ever lost your textbook?

   Melissa Yes, I have. I left it on a bus.

   ___*Melissa hasn't ever forgotten to study for a test.*___

   ___*She has lost her textbook.*___

2. **Luis** Have you ever had trouble concentrating on your homework?

   Franco Yes!

   Luis Have you ever done the wrong homework?

   Franco No, I don't think so.

   _____

   _____

3. **Maria** Have you ever read a newspaper in English?

   Rose Yes, I have.

   Maria Have you ever tried to speak English with your neighbors?

   Rose No, I haven't. But I want to!

   _____

   _____

4. **Ken** Have you ever asked your teacher for extra help?

   Andy No, but I should ask for more help!

   Ken Have you ever been late for class?

   Andy Well, yes, sometimes.

   _____

   _____

Check your answers. See page 131.

1 Read the article. Answer the questions.

Strategies for Learning New Words

Have you ever felt discouraged because there are so many new words to learn in English? Have you tried to set goals for learning new words? Here are some ideas to help you practice and remember vocabulary.

Strategy #1: Keep a vocabulary notebook.
Buy a small notebook. Take it with you everywhere. When you see new words around you in the street, on an advertisement, or in a newspaper, write the new words in your notebook. Use clues to guess the meanings. At the end of the day, use your dictionary to check the meanings. Write an example sentence or draw a picture to help you remember the new words.

Strategy #2: Make vocabulary cards.
Have you ever felt bored waiting in line or taking the bus? Use the time to practice vocabulary. Choose five words from your English class or from a newspaper or magazine. Write each word on a small card. Write the word on one side of the card. Then write the definition or a translation on the other side. Test yourself on the definitions.

Strategy #3: Use new words in conversations every day.
Choose one new word from your notebook or vocabulary cards every day. Try to use it in a conversation some time during the day with your friends, classmates, family, or with your teacher. Using the words you learn will help you remember them.

1. What is the reading about?

   The reading is about strategies for learning new words.

2. What are the three strategies described in this article?

   1. _____

   2. _____

   3. _____

3. If you write a new word on one side of a card and write the definition on the other side, what strategy are you using?

   _____

Check your answers. See page 131.

2 Circle the answers. Use the information in Exercise 1.

1. The article says you can use *all* of
   these strategies _____ .
   a. in class
   b. every day *(circled)*
   c. on the bus
   d. with pictures

2. The article says these strategies
   should help you to _____ new words.
   a. draw
   b. write
   c. translate
   d. remember

3. The article says you should use
   _____ to check definitions.
   a. a dictionary
   b. a notebook
   c. an index card
   d. an advertisement

4. The article says you can practice
   using new words when _____ .
   a. watching TV
   b. talking to friends
   c. listening to the radio
   d. reading a newspaper

3 Make sentences. Match the sentence parts. Use the information in Exercise 1.

1. You can draw pictures __c__
2. You can use new words _____
3. You can look at vocabulary cards _____
4. You should guess the meaning first _____
5. You should write definitions _____

a. and use a dictionary later.
b. on the back of vocabulary cards.
c. in your vocabulary notebook.
d. when you talk to friends.
e. when you are waiting in line.

4 Look at the **bold** words. Write a word from the box with a similar meaning.

clues	gestures	plan	practice	set	strategies

1. The article suggests some easy **methods** for learning new words.

   ___strategies___

2. I need to **decide on** a few goals for learning English.

   _____

3. Have you made a **decision** to help you reach your goals?

   _____

4. I need to **use** new words every day to help me remember them.

   _____

5. Certain **information** in a sentence can help you guess the meaning.

   _____

6. **Hand movements** can sometimes help to explain the meaning.

   _____

Check your answers. See page 131.

Writing

1 Complete the chart.

Ask questions in class every day.	Underline new words with colored pens.
Listen to the radio.	Use new words in everyday conversation.
Look up new words in a dictionary.	Watch movies in English.
Read newspapers in English.	Watch the news in English.
Talk to people at work in English.	

Listening strategies	Speaking strategies	Reading strategies
Listen to the radio.		

2 Read Omar's journal. Answer the questions.

I want to improve my reading in English. One strategy is to read newspapers or magazines in English. For example, I'm going to read a newspaper article in English every day. I'm also going to use colored pens to underline new words. For example, I'll use a yellow pen for new and difficult words and a blue pen when I can guess the meaning. Another strategy is to use my dictionary more often. I will choose five words I don't know each day and check the meanings in my dictionary.

1. What is Omar's first strategy for improving his reading? Give an example.

   Omar's first strategy is to read newspapers or magazines in English.

   He is going to read a newspaper article in English every day.

2. What is Omar's second strategy for improving his reading? Give an example.

   _____

   _____

3. What is Omar's third strategy for improving his reading? Give an example.

   _____

   _____

Check your answers. See page 131.

3 Read the strategies. Write the number of the strategy next to the example.

Strategy 1: Guess the meaning of new words.

Strategy 2: Use one new word every day.

Strategy 3: Make a vocabulary notebook.

Strategy 4: Review new words after class.

_2_ 1. I'll write the new word in a sentence and send it in an e-mail to my friend.

____ 2. I'll write three new words in my notebook every day.

____ 3. I'll make vocabulary cards and look at them on the bus.

____ 4. I can look at the pictures and sentences around a new word and figure out the meaning.

4 Write a paragraph about four strategies for learning new words. Give one example for each strategy. Use the strategies and examples in Exercise 3.

I have learned some useful strategies for learning new words.

_____

_____

_____

_____

_____

_____

_____

_____

_____

_____

_____

_____

_____

_____

Check your answers. See page 132.

1 Complete the sentences.

answer	look	make	read	skim	spend	worry

Test-taking tips

1. _____Read_____ the directions carefully.

2. _____ the whole test before you start.

3. _____ the most difficult questions at the end.

4. Don't _____ too much time on one question.

5. Don't _____ if the other students finish before you.

6. _____ sure you have answered all questions on the test.

7. Don't _____ at other students' tests.

2 Which tips did these students need to follow? Write the number of the tip from Exercise 1.

1. I spent 20 minutes on the first question, and I didn't have time to finish the other questions. Tip _4_

2. Everyone finished before me, and I started to worry. Tip ____

3. I forgot to answer some of the questions. Tip ____

4. I tried to look at another student's test, and I failed the test. Tip ____

5. I didn't know the test had three parts. I only finished two parts. Tip ____

6. I spent too much time on the difficult questions. I wasn't able to answer the easy questions. Tip ____

7. I circled the answers, but the directions said: "Underline the answers." Tip ____

Check your answers. See page 132.

3 Read the tips. Answer the questions.

> # Five tips to help you prepare for a test
>
> 1. Ask for or find some practice tests. Study them.
> 2. Take a practice test, and time yourself.
> 3. Write the most difficult questions on index cards. Study them in your free time.
> 4. Use the Internet to find advice about taking tests.
> 5. Get a good night's sleep, and eat a healthy breakfast before the test.

1. Which tip will help you finish the test on time? Tip _2_

2. Which tip will help you understand the test? Tip ____

3. Which tip will help you feel awake? Tip ____

4. Which tip will help you to find other tips? Tip ____

5. Which tip will help you to remember difficult information? Tip ____

4 Look at the bar graph. It is about the strategies used last week by students in an intermediate ESL class to help them learn English. Answer the questions.

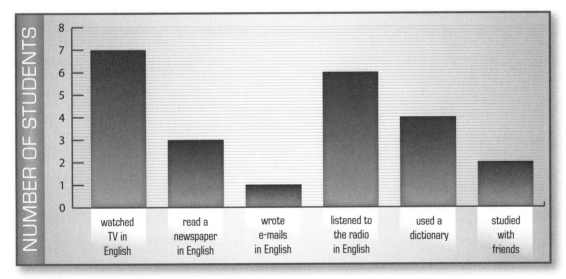

1. How many students watched TV in English last week? _7_

2. How many students listened to the radio in English last week? ____

3. How many students wrote e-mails in English last week? ____

4. How many students read a newspaper in English last week? ____

5. How many students studied with friends last week? ____

6. How many students used a dictionary last week? ____

Check your answers. See page 132.

Friends and family

1 Complete the paragraph.

| borrow | broken | came over | complain | favor | noisy |

I Owe You One

My neighbor Amy ___*came over*___ yesterday to ask a
1

_____ . Her light was _____ , and
2   3

it was too high for her to reach. She wanted to _____
4

my ladder. We had a cup of coffee and started to talk about our other

neighbors. Two weeks ago, they had a party, and Amy told them the music

was too loud. Then, last weekend, they had another party. Amy couldn't

sleep because they were too _____ . I said she should
5

_____ to the building manager, and I gave her the phone
6

number. Then I helped her carry my ladder to her apartment.

"Rita, thanks for your help," she said. "I owe you one!"

2 Circle the answers. Use the information in Exercise 1.

1. Amy asked Rita for a ____ .
   a. ladder
   b. new light
   c. phone number
   d. cup of coffee

2. Amy couldn't sleep because ____ .
   a. her light was broken
   b. the neighbors had a party
   c. she needed to call the manager
   d. she needed to borrow a ladder

3. Amy ____ Rita's help.
   a. doesn't need
   b. doesn't want
   c. complains about
   d. really appreciates

4. Amy owes Rita a ____ .
   a. favor
   b. ladder
   c. phone number
   d. cup of coffee

Check your answers. See page 132.

3 Complete the sentences.

appreciates	come over	favor	noisy
borrow	complained	noise	owe

1. Mary hasn't read this book. She is going to _____*borrow*_____ it from me.

2. The neighbors are not quiet. They are _____ all the time.

3. Meg thanked Tina for her help. She always _____ Tina's help.

4. I borrowed ten dollars from you. Here's two dollars, so I now _____ you eight dollars.

5. My neighbors were so noisy last night. I _____ to the apartment manager.

6. Our old washing machine makes a lot of _____ . Our new washing machine is quiet.

7. Could you do me a _____ and babysit my children tonight?

8. My daughter wants her friend to _____ , but I said no. It's a school night.

4 Circle the correct word.

1. Rita **lent** / **borrowed** a ladder to Amy.

2. Amy **lent** / **borrowed** a ladder from Rita.

3. My friend **lent** / **borrowed** a book from me.

4. I **lent** / **borrowed** a book to my friend.

5. Pete **lent** / **borrowed** his bicycle to Mark.

6. Mark **lent** / **borrowed** a bicycle from Pete.

5 Complete the sentences. Use *lend* or *borrow*.

1. Could you _____*lend*_____ me some money? I want to buy a cup of coffee.

2. I can't _____ you my cell phone right now. It's broken.

3. Could I _____ your dictionary? I forgot how to spell this word.

4. Do you want to _____ my umbrella? It's raining outside.

5. He didn't _____ my jacket, so he was very cold.

6. I sometimes have to _____ money to my daughter. I hope she finds a job soon.

Check your answers. See page 132.

Because and *because of*

Study the explanation on page 128.

1 Make sentences. Match the sentence parts.

1. Stan borrowed some money __c__   a. because of his job.
2. Dan travels a lot ____   b. because she had a big test.
3. Alfredo and Maria were late ____   c. because he wants to buy a car.
4. Dolores studied for three hours ____   d. because his window was broken.
5. Tran called the building manager ____   e. because of a flat tire.

2 Circle *because* or *because of*.

1. Ana couldn't sleep **because** / **because of** the baby was crying.

2. I couldn't go to work **because** / **because of** my car broke down.

3. We didn't go out **because** / **because of** the bad weather.

4. Tanya needed a ladder **because** / **because of** the broken light.

5. Joseph couldn't take a vacation **because** / **because of** his busy work schedule.

6. Marietta didn't come to class **because** / **because of** she had a bad headache.

3 Rewrite the sentences. Use the words in parentheses.

1. We couldn't sleep *because it was noisy*. (the noise)

   We couldn't sleep because of the noise.

2. We couldn't play soccer *because it was raining*. (the rain)

   _____

3. They were late for the appointment *because there were a lot of cars*. (the traffic)

   _____

4. Reyna stayed at home *because she had the flu*. (the flu)

   _____

5. Sam stayed up late *because he watched the basketball game*. (the basketball game)

   _____

6. Beatriz moved to this country *because her children live here*. (her children)

   _____

Check your answers. See page 132.

4 Complete the sentences. Use *because* or *because of*.

1. Teresa couldn't sleep last night _____*because*_____ she had a headache.
2. Keizo couldn't lock his door _____ he lost his keys.
3. We moved to California _____ my husband's job.
4. William couldn't drive his car _____ the broken door.
5. Karen likes her neighborhood _____ it is safe at night.

5 Complete the sentences. Use *because* or *because of* and words from the box.

he was sick	it was her son's birthday	the smoke
it was closed	the rain	there were so many people

1. They couldn't go to the supermarket *because it was closed* _____ .
2. They couldn't play baseball _____ .
3. She made a cake _____ .
4. My neighbor called 911 _____ .
5. He couldn't go to school _____ .
6. We had to wait a long time _____ .

Check your answers. See page 132.

Lesson C *Enough* and *too*

Study the explanation on page 128.

1 Write the opposites.

close	hot	small	strong	tall	young

1. cold ___*hot*___
2. short _____
3. big _____

4. weak _____
5. far _____
6. old _____

2 Complete the sentences. Use the adjectives in Exercise 1.

1. The water is ___*hot*___ enough to make coffee.
2. He isn't _____ enough to reach the ceiling.
3. They're not _____ enough to lift the box.
4. The car is too _____ for five people.
5. He is too _____ to get married.
6. The train station isn't _____ enough to walk.

3 Complete the sentences. Use the correct adjective and *too* or *enough*.

1. She's ___*too young*___ .
2. She's not ___*old enough*___ .

3. He's _____ .
4. He's not _____ .

5. It's _____ .
6. It's not _____ .

Check your answers. See page 132.

4 Complete the sentences. Use *too* or *not . . . enough* with the word in parentheses.

1. **A** I don't want to live in the city anymore. It's _____ *too noisy* _____ .
   (noisy)

   B I agree. It's _____ *not quiet enough* _____ .
   (quiet)

2. **A** The rent for this apartment is _____ .
   (expensive)

   B You're right. It's _____ .
   (cheap)

3. **A** We need a new house. Our house is _____ .
   (small)

   B That's true. Our house is _____ .
   (big)

4. **A** I don't like this exercise. It's _____ .
   (difficult)

   B I agree. It's _____ .
   (easy)

5. **A** I want to quit my job. It's _____ .
   (boring)

   B You've complained to me before that your job is _____ .
   (interesting)

6. **A** My daughter wants to take a trip by herself. She's _____ .
   (young)

   B I agree. She's _____ .
   (old)

5 Complete the sentences. Use the correct adjective and *too* or *enough*.

big	expensive	experienced	high	old	strong	tall	weak	young

1. I have five children. This house isn't _____ *big enough* _____ for us.

2. James is six feet 10 inches. He's _____ to reach
   the ceiling.

3. My daughter is six months old. She's not _____ to talk.

4. The books are on the top shelf. They're _____ to reach.

5. This box is not very heavy. I'm _____ to carry it.

6. Meredith is 14 years old. She's _____ to drive.

7. My husband hasn't finished his training. He's not _____
   to be an engineer.

8. We need to buy a used car. A new car is _____ for us.

9. I need some help! I'm _____ to lift this TV.

Check your answers. See page 132.

1 Read the story. Correct the information in the sentences.

MY NEIGHBORHOOD

People sometimes ask me about my neighborhood. Is it nice? Is it safe? My answer is that I'm very lucky to have nice neighbors. They are very friendly and kind. For example, they help me with shopping when I feel too sick to go out. They watch out for my house when I am away. Once a month, we get together to talk about any problems.

Last week, my neighbors saw some teenagers near my house. They were painting graffiti on a wall. My neighbors shouted at them, and they ran away. The next day, my neighbors came over with some brushes and some paint. We painted over the graffiti together, and the teens haven't come back. I am so happy that I have such nice neighbors. Because of my neighbors, this neighborhood is a safe place to live.

1. The writer doesn't like to spend time with her neighbors.

   The writer gets together with her neighbors once a month.

2. The writer's neighbors painted graffiti.

   _____

3. My neighbors talked to the teenagers, and they walked away.

   _____

4. The writer's neighborhood is not safe.

   _____

Check your answers. See page 132.

2 Circle the answers. Use the information in Exercise 1.

1. What is the main idea of the
   first paragraph?
   a. The writer's neighbors watch her house.
   b. The writer's neighbors talk every month.
   (c.) The writer's neighbors are friendly.
   d. The writer's neighbors are too noisy.

2. The writer gives examples to show that _____ .
   a. her neighbors are nice people
   b. her neighbors talk too much
   c. she has very few neighbors
   d. she has a lot of neighbors

3. What did the neighbors see?
   a. teenagers talking
   b. teenagers painting graffiti
   c. teenagers breaking a window
   d. teenagers breaking into the
      writer's house

4. What did the neighbors do?
   a. They ran away.
   b. They called the police.
   c. They stayed in their houses.
   d. They shouted at the teenagers.

3 Complete the sentences.

break into	get into	get together	goes off	run away	watch out for

1. You can _____ *get into* _____ my car and wait for me. Here's the key.

2. When do you want to _____ again?

3. My neighbors _____ my dog when I'm on vacation.

4. My smoke alarm sometimes _____ when I am cooking.

5. I close the windows so my cat can't _____ .

6. Someone tried to _____ my car yesterday, so I called
   the police.

4 Look at the **bold** words. Write verbs from Exercise 3 with a similar meaning.

1. The men tried to **escape** when they saw the police car. _____ *run away* _____

2. I **take care of** my neighbor's children in the afternoon. _____

3. My friends and I often **meet** at a coffee shop after class. _____

4. My alarm clock **makes a loud noise** at 6:00 every morning. _____

5. My shoes are very dirty. I shouldn't **enter** your car. _____

6. Someone tried to **enter** my home last night, so I called the police. _____

Check your answers. See page 133.

Writing

1 Read the letter. Label the parts of the letter.

| problem | request | signature | today's date |

1. ___today's date___

July 15, 2009

Century Building Management
1000 Chestnut Street
Miami, FL 33127

To Whom It May Concern:

2. _____

My name is Nazmi Akerjee. I live at 310 Walnut Street in Apartment 5. I am writing because the hallway outside my apartment has a broken light. I tried to fix it, but my ladder is not tall enough to reach it. The hallway is not safe at night because of the broken light.

3. _____

Could you please come as soon as possible to fix the light? Thank you in advance for your help.

Sincerely,

Nazmi Akerjee

4. _____

Nazmi Akerjee

2 Circle *T* (true) or *F* (false). Use the information in Exercise 1.

1. Nazmi knows the name of the person to whom she is writing.   T   (F)
2. Nazmi's address is 310 Chestnut Street, Apartment 5.   T   F
3. The broken light is inside Nazmi's apartment.   T   F
4. Nazmi feels that her hallway is not safe at night.   T   F
5. Nazmi wants someone to fix the light.   T   F
6. Nazmi tried to fix the light.   T   F
7. The ladder is tall enough to reach the light.   T   F
8. Century Building Management is at 1000 Chestnut Street.   T   F

Check your answers. See page 133.

3 Complete the sentences.

advance	because	because of	soon	too

1. Could you please send a repair person as _____ *soon* _____ as possible?

2. I am writing _____ my window is broken.

3. It is _____ cold for me to sleep in the apartment.

4. Thank you in _____ for fixing the problem.

5. _____ the broken window, my apartment is very cold.

4 Write a letter of complaint about a broken window. Use the information in Exercise 3.

_____

Prestige Apartments
286 10th Street
Burlington, VT 05401

_____:

My name is _____

_____

_____

_____

_____

_____

_____

_____

_____

Sincerely,

_____

Check your answers. See page 133.

Another view

1 Read the questions. Look at the ad. Circle the answers.

Hillside Hospital Seeks Four Volunteers
Start immediately!

Hours: 1:00 p.m.–7:00 p.m., three afternoons a week

Job Duties: Greet visitors with a smile and take them to patients' rooms. Serve tea, coffee, and cold drinks to visitors. Play games with patients, and bring books to their rooms.

Requirements: 18 years old or older. Seniors welcome to apply. Must be friendly, helpful, and patient. Teamwork skills a plus.

Send resume and letter of interest to:
Volunteer Division
Hillside Hospital
1200 Hillside Avenue
Los Angeles, CA 90027
No phone calls please.

1. Volunteers must be _____ years old.
   a. over 18
   b. over 65
   c. under 18
   d. under 65

2. How many hours do volunteers have to work a day?
   a. one
   b. three
   c. six
   d. seven

3. Which statement is NOT true?
   a. Volunteers should be patient.
   b. Volunteers should be very friendly.
   c. Volunteers should be experienced nurses.
   d. Volunteers should like meeting people.

4. What will a volunteer at the hospital do?
   a. assist nurses
   b. assist visitors
   c. give medicine
   d. serve food

5. How many days a week do volunteers have to work?
   a. one
   b. three
   c. four
   d. seven

6. Which statement is true?
   a. Volunteers must prefer to work alone.
   b. Volunteers must like meeting people.
   c. Volunteers must call to apply.
   d. Volunteers must like children.

Check your answers. See page 133.

2 Read the ads. Match the ads and the sentences.

1. Tracy has too many cans of food at home. _B_

2. Alina thinks there is too much trash in the park. ____

3. Bettina loves reading stories to children. ____

4. Teresa likes to exercise and work with young people. ____

5. Petra loves cats and dogs. ____

6. Tony likes talking to older people. ____

3 Complete the sentences. Use the information in Exercise 2.

experienced	far	old	strong	young

1. Alina is only 15 years old. She is too _____*young*_____ to work at the senior care center.

2. Tracy volunteers every year. She is an _____ volunteer.

3. Petra is 18. She is _____ enough to work at the animal shelter.

4. Bettina feels sick today. She is not _____ enough to do the Neighborhood Watch trash clean up.

5. Tony doesn't live close to the high school. He lives too _____ away to be a soccer volunteer.

Check your answers. See page 133.

Lesson A *Get ready*

1 Complete the paragraph.

| advice | diet | exercise | gained | pressure | weight |

Dear Alice,

My husband Alex is an office assistant. He drives to work every day. He works on the tenth floor, and he always takes the elevator. His _____*diet*_____ is not very healthy. For example, for lunch, he usually
1
eats pizza or a hamburger and fries. On the weekend, he often eats a lot of ice cream and cookies. He doesn't _____ very much. In fact, he usually takes a walk
2
only once a week on Saturday. He never rides his bike. He is worried because his blood _____ is high, and he has _____ 15 pounds. He knows he
3   4
has to lose some _____ . He has also been very tired lately. What should
5
he do?

Worried in Seattle

Dear Worried in Seattle,

Your husband needs to make an appointment to see his doctor so that he can ask the doctor for some _____ .
6
Alice

2 Circle the answers. Use the information in Exercise 1.

1. Alex always ____ .
   a. takes the elevator
   b. walks up the stairs

2. Alex does not ____ .
   a. take walks
   b. exercise enough

3. Alex's blood pressure is too ____ .
   a. high
   b. low

4. Alex is worried because ____ .
   a. he never rides his bike
   b. he has gained weight

5. Alex needs to ____ .
   a. sleep less
   b. change his diet

6. Alice says Alex needs to ____ .
   a. change his job
   b. talk to his doctor

Check your answers. See page 133.

3 Complete the chart.

check your weight	eat fish
drink a lot of soda	gain 20 pounds
eat a lot of hamburgers	go to bed late
eat breakfast	ride a bicycle
eat cookies	take a walk every day

Healthy activities	Unhealthy activities
check your weight	

4 Complete the sentences.

| advice | diet | exercise | health | medication | tired | weight |

1. **A** Pat eats too many hamburgers. He needs to change his _____*diet*_____ .

   B I know.

2. **A** Alex has high blood pressure. He needs to take _____ .

   B That's too bad.

3. **A** I've gained 20 pounds. I need to lose _____ .

   B You should try going to the gym three times a week.

4. **A** Ali sits at work all day.

   B He needs to _____ regularly.

5. **A** I really want to stay healthy.

   B Then you need to follow your doctor's _____ .

6. **A** My _____ has always been good, but I haven't been feeling
   well lately.

   B I think you should see a doctor.

7. **A** I feel so _____ lately!

   B Are you getting enough sleep? How is your diet?

Check your answers. See page 133.

Study the chart and explanation on page 124. For a list of irregular verbs,
turn to page 127.

1 Complete the paragraph. Use the present perfect.

be	eat	exercise	gain	give	go	start

I ___have gained___ weight recently, so I have decided
      1
to change my diet and get in shape. I _____
                                                        2
up potato chips, and I _____ not _____ any pizza
                                    3
recently. I _____ to eat more salad and fruit.
                    4
I _____ at the gym three times this week
        5
already. I can see that I am losing weight, and I'm sure
my blood pressure _____ down. I feel healthier,
                            6
and I _____ not _____ tired in a long time.
            7

2 Write sentences. Use the present perfect.

1. You / not / exercise / this week

   You haven't exercised this week.

2. Paul / gain weight / recently

   _____

3. Ray and Louisa / lose weight / recently

   _____

4. Alicia / be unhappy / lately

   _____

5. My blood pressure / go up / recently

   _____

6. Greg / not / visit a dentist / recently

   _____

7. Sarah / give up / desserts / lately

   _____

Check your answers. See page 133.

3 Write sentences about Annette. Use the present perfect with *recently*.

> ### Annette's Goals for November
>
> 1. Check blood pressure.
> 2. Go to the gym. ✓
> 3. Eat more fruits and vegetables. ✓
> 4. Sleep eight hours a day. ✓
> 5. Take vitamins.

1. _Annette hasn't checked her blood pressure recently._

2. _____

3. _____

4. _____

5. _____

4 Write questions and answers. Use the present perfect.

1. Bill / lose weight / recently

   A _Has Bill lost weight recently_ ?

   B No, _he hasn't_ .

2. Tina and Mario / give up desserts / recently

   A _____ ?

   B Yes, _____ .

3. you / check your blood pressure / lately

   A _____ ?

   B No, _____ .

4. Barbara / sleep much / lately

   A _____ ?

   B Yes, _____.

5. Lisa / start taking vitamins / recently

   A _____ ?

   B No, _____ .

Check your answers. See page 133.

Lesson C Used to

Study the chart and explanation on page 125.

1 Circle *use* or *used*.

1. Did Angie (use)/ **used** to have high blood pressure?

2. They **use** / **used** to drink a lot of coffee.

3. Tia and Arturo **use** / **used** to go to the gym every weekend.

4. Did Wesley **use** / **used** to drive to work?

5. We **use** / **used** to eat hamburgers and fries.

6. Did you **use** / **used** to feel tired all the time?

2 Complete the sentences. Use *used to* or *use to*.

1. When I was a teenager, I ____used to____ play soccer.

2. Did you _____ exercise a lot when you were young?

3. In my country, I _____ eat rice every day.

4. When I was a child, I _____ drink milk every morning.

5. Did you _____ watch TV when you were a child?

6. I _____ get up late every day, but now I get up early.

3 Complete the paragraph. Use *used to* or the simple present tense.

Samantha _____*used to eat*_____ a lot of chocolate and ice cream,
           1. eat

but now she _____*eats*_____ a lot of fruit and vegetables. She
            2. eat

_____ vitamins every day. She _____ only
   3. take   4. exercise

once a week, but now she _____ to the gym three times a
                              5. go

week. She _____ to work, but now she _____
              6. drive   7. ride

a bike. She _____ a lot of coffee, but now she
                 8. drink

_____ tea or fruit juice. She _____ tired all
   9. drink   10. feel

the time, but now she _____ a lot of energy. Samantha has
                           11. have

changed her habits and feels much better now.

Check your answers. See page 133.

4 Read the chart. Write sentences about Emilia.

Before	Now
1. Stay up until 2:00 a.m.	Go to bed at 10:00 p.m.
2. Eat meat every day	Eat fish twice a week
3. Go straight home after work	Go to the gym three times a week
4. Eat a lot of fatty foods	Eat salad and vegetables
5. Skip breakfast	Eat fruit and yogurt for breakfast

1. _Emilia used to stay up until 2:00 a.m., but now she goes to bed at 10:00 p.m._

2. _____

3. _____

4. _____

5. _____

5 Write questions and answers about what Emilia used to do.
Use the information in Exercise 4.

1. Emilia / stay up until 2:00 a.m.

   A _Did Emilia use to stay up until 2:00 a.m._ ?

   B _Yes, she did_ .

2. she / eat meat every day

   A _____ ?

   B _____ .

3. she / go to the gym three times a week

   A _____ ?

   B _____ .

Check your answers. See page 134.

1 Read the article. Answer the questions.

THREE **HEALTHFUL** HERBS

Many herbal plants are easy to grow. You can use them in cooking and to prevent illness. You can grow thyme, lavender, and mint in a garden or in your home.

Thyme is a small herbal plant. You can use it in cooking and as a medicine. The leaves are gray-green, and the flowers are usually purple, white, or pink. Many people use thyme to cook chicken and fish. You can also dry the leaves and make tea with them. Thyme tea with honey is very good for a cough or a sore throat.

Lavender is a popular garden plant with silver-green leaves and tiny purple flowers. The flowers have a beautiful smell. You can use the dried flowers to keep clothes and sheets fresh. You can use lavender when cooking meat, and you can make tea from the dried flowers for headaches and high blood pressure. Some people use lavender oil in their bath to help them relax.

Mint is a healthful plant that grows quickly. You can use the leaves in salads and with meat or fish. You can use the fresh or dried leaves to make tea. It helps with indigestion and upset stomachs. Add sugar to iced mint tea for a healthful and delicious summer drink.

Use thyme, lavender, and mint to stay healthy and prevent illness.

1. Which of the herbs in the article is good for treating indigestion?
   Mint is good for treating indigestion.

2. Which of the herbs in the article is good for treating headaches?
   _____

3. Which of the herbs in the article is good for treating stomachaches?
   _____

4. What illnesses can thyme tea help treat?
   _____

Check your answers. See page 134.

2 Complete the chart. Use the information in Exercise 1.

Name of plant	Use it to make . . .	Use it to cook . . .	Use it to treat . . .
Thyme	tea		
Lavender			
Mint			

3 Complete the sentences. Use the information in Exercise 1.

| digest | digestion | herbal | prevent | treat | treatment |

1. I'm having problems with my _____ digestion _____ . I think I'll drink some mint tea.
2. Some people use thyme tea as a _____ for sore throats.
3. Lavender can help _____ high blood pressure.
4. You can use mint to make delicious _____ tea.
5. Mint can help you _____ your food.
6. Some people use lavender tea to _____ headaches.

4 Write *adjective*, *noun*, or *verb*.

1. digestive: _____ *adjective* _____
2. prevention: _____
3. treat: _____
4. herbs: _____
5. digest: _____
6. prevent: _____
7. treatment: _____

Check your answers. See page 134.

1 Read about sage. Answer the questions.

> Sage is another popular herbal plant used for cooking and medicine. It is easy to grow in your garden. It has green-gray leaves and purple flowers. You can make tea from the leaves to treat sore throats and breathing problems. I also use it to add flavor to meat or vegetables. I sometimes use sage tea as a mouthwash, too.

1. What is sage used for? *cooking and medicine* _____

2. What does it look like? _____

3. What health problems can you treat with sage? _____

4. How can you use it in cooking? _____

5. How else can you use it? _____

2 Complete the paragraph. Use the information in the chart.

Plant name	rosemary
Grows	in the garden or in your home
Description	sharp, narrow leaves
Treats	headaches
Cooking uses	adds flavor to meat or oil

> _____*Rosemary*_____ is my favorite herbal plant. It is widely used for
>   1
>
> cooking and medicine. It is easy to grow in your _____ .
>   2
>
> It has _____ . You can use the leaves to treat
>   3
>
> _____ . I also use it in cooking to _____ .
>   4   5

Check your answers. See page 134.

3 Read the chart. Answer the questions.

Plant name	aloe vera
History	people have used it for 6,000 years
Grows	in hot, dry places
Description	• long, spiky leaves • leaves have juice inside them
Treats	• burns • insect bites • dry skin
Used in	• skin creams and lotions • shampoos • soaps

1. Where does the aloe vera grow? _in hot, dry places_ _____

2. What kind of leaves does it have? _____

3. What problems can you treat with aloe vera? _____

4. What products have aloe vera in them? _____

4 Write a paragraph about aloe vera. Use the information in Exercise 3.

People have used aloe vera for thousands of years. _____

_____

_____

_____

_____

_____

_____

_____

_____

_____

_____

_____

Check your answers. See page 134.

Another view

1 Read the questions. Look at the form. Circle the answers.

Medical History Form

1. What is the reason for your visit?

Problem   Date problem began
_____ allergies _____   _____ 3 weeks ago _____

2. Have you ever had any of the following?

☑ allergies	☐ back pain	☑ headaches	☑ high blood pressure
☐ arthritis	☐ chest pains	☐ heart attack	☑ high cholesterol
☑ asthma	☐ diabetes	☐ heart disease	☐ tuberculosis

3. Please list all medications, including vitamins and herbal supplements.
_____ Vitamin C, garlic pills, and aspirin _____

4. List any other major illnesses, injuries, or surgeries you have had in the last year.
_____

The above information is correct to the best of my knowledge.

Signature _____ Eva Hernandez _____   Date _____ August 25, 2009 _____

1. Eva went to the doctor because of _____ .
   a. arthritis
   b. allergies
   c. diabetes
   d. back pain

2. Eva does not take _____ .
   a. aspirin
   b. garlic pills
   c. Vitamin C
   d. Vitamin D

3. In the past, Eva has had _____ .
   a. chest pains
   b. tuberculosis
   c. heart disease
   d. high cholesterol

4. In the past, Eva has not had _____ .
   a. asthma
   b. headaches
   c. heart disease
   d. high blood pressure

Check your answers. See page 134.

2 Match the pictures with the advice.

1

a. **Exercise regularly.**

b. **Start taking vitamins.**

c. **Give up desserts.**

d. **See a doctor.**

2

3

4

3 Look at the word maps. Cross out the words or phrases that are different.

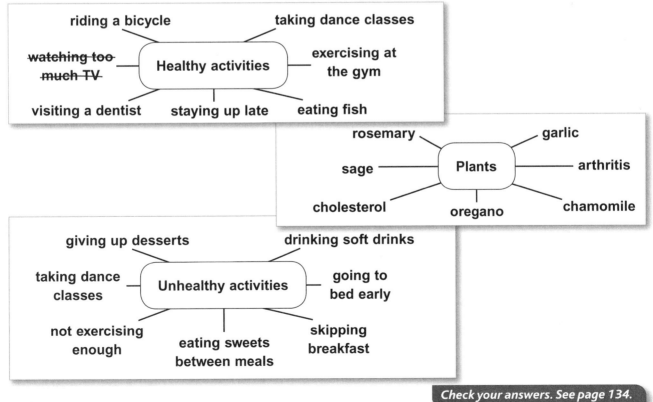

riding a bicycle

taking dance classes

~~watching too much TV~~ — **Healthy activities**

exercising at the gym

visiting a dentist   staying up late   eating fish

rosemary   garlic

sage — **Plants** — arthritis

cholesterol   oregano   chamomile

giving up desserts   drinking soft drinks

taking dance classes — **Unhealthy activities**

going to bed early

not exercising enough   eating sweets between meals   skipping breakfast

Check your answers. See page 134.

Around town

1 Read the ads. Match the ads with the sentences.

1. Rick and Becky can't afford to spend a lot on entertainment. __*B*__

2. Bill and Margie want to get some exercise and be outside. _____

3. Maria's daughter loves books. _____

4. The weather is bad, so Lin wants to do something interesting indoors. _____

2 Complete the sentences.

admission	afford	concerts	events	exhibits	storytelling

1. We usually check the newspaper for community _____*events*_____ .

2. I love music. I like going to rock _____ .

3. We don't have any money. We can't _____ expensive tickets.

4. The garden tour is free. There is no _____ fee.

5. My children love stories. They love listening to _____ at the library.

6. My wife loves art. She often goes to art _____ .

Check your answers. See page 134.

3 Read the conversation. Circle the answers.

A Yan, do you have any plans for Saturday?

B No, Lin, not yet.

A There's a free concert in the park on Saturday afternoon. Do you want to go?

B That sounds good. What time does it start?

A It starts at 3:00. And there's a new art exhibit at the museum.

B Wow! We have so many options. What time does the museum open?

A 10:00. And it's free admission.

B OK. Let's meet at the museum at 11:00. We'll have lunch in the museum café, and then we'll go to the concert.

A It's a plan!

1. Yan and Lin are _____ .
   a. going shopping
   b. discussing music
   c. choosing a good restaurant
   d. planning their weekend

2. They are going to go to _____ .
   a. a park and a concert
   b. a park and a movie
   c. an art exhibit and a concert
   d. an art exhibit and a movie

3. First, Yan and Lin will _____ .
   a. walk in the park
   b. eat lunch at a café
   c. go to a free concert
   d. meet at an art museum

4. The museum opens at _____ .
   a. 9:00 a.m.
   b. 10:00 a.m.
   c. 11:00 a.m.
   d. 3:00 p.m.

5. Which statement is true?
   a. The concert tickets are not cheap.
   b. There is no admission fee for the concert.
   c. Admission to the museum is not free.
   d. Admission to the museum is expensive.

6. Yan and Lin plan to spend _____ .
   a. no money at all
   b. no money on food
   c. some money on food
   d. some money on entertainment

Check your answers. See page 134.

Verbs + infinitives

Study the chart and explanation on page 123.

1 Complete the sentences. Use the infinitive.

come home	eat	go	meet	see	take

A Nina, where have you decided

_____*to go*_____ this afternoon?

B I'm going to the art museum with my friend Gabe.

A What do you want _____2_____ ?

B There's a new exhibit on American paintings. I think

it's going to be great.

A Where have you agreed _____3_____ Gabe?

B Outside the art museum at 1:00.

A Where do you plan _____4_____ ?

B We'll eat lunch at home.

A Can you afford _____5_____ a taxi?

B No, we'll take the subway.

A What time do you expect _____6_____ ?

B I should be home before 6:00.

2 Complete the sentences. Use the infinitive.

1. Nina doesn't _____*want to ride*_____ her bike this afternoon.
   (want / ride)
2. She _____ at home.
   (plan / eat)
3. She _____ Gabe at the museum.
   (intend / meet)
4. She doesn't _____ a taxi.
   (need / take)
5. She _____ home by 6:00.
   (expects / be)
6. She _____ something from the gift shop.
   (would like / buy)
7. She _____ something that is not too expensive.
   (hope / find)

Check your answers. See page 134.

3 Rewrite the sentences. Use the verb in parentheses and an infinitive.

1. Tony will visit his family every year. (promise)

   Tony promises to visit his family every year.

2. Lee will finish work early tonight. (expect)

   _____

3. I'll go to Florida this winter. (plan)

   _____

4. Shin will buy some concert tickets tomorrow. (intend)

   _____

5. We will visit our daughter in California next month. (hope)

   _____

6. Paul will not go to the beach this weekend. (refuse)

   _____

7. I will meet my friends on my birthday. (want)

   _____

8. I will take a trip with my family next year. (would like)

   _____

4 Complete the sentences about Chris's goals.

CHRIS'S GOALS					
January	**February**	**March**	**April**	**May**	**June**
Watch less TV	Go to an art museum	Visit relatives more often	Walk to work every day	Give up desserts	Buy organic vegetables

1. (plan) In January, _Chris plans to watch less TV_ .
2. (intend) In February, _____ .
3. (want) In March, _____ .
4. (plan) In April, _____ .
5. (would like) In May, _____ .
6. (hope) In June, _____ .

Check your answers. See page 134.

Study the list of irregular verbs on page 127.

1 Complete the sentences. Use the present perfect.

1. Have Sue and Martin ____*seen*____ that movie already?
   (see)

2. Has Tim _____ dinner yet?
   (make)

3. We haven't _____ the newspaper yet.
   (read)

4. Have you _____ the credit card bill already?
   (pay)

5. My brother has already _____ his ticket.
   (buy)

6. Have the children _____ their homework yet?
   (do)

2 Complete the sentences. Use *already* or *yet*.

1. It's 8:00 p.m.

   The violin concert ____*hasn't started yet*____ .
   (start)

2. It's 6:30 p.m.

   The coffee shop _____ .
   (close)

3. It's 7:00 p.m.

   The movie _____ .
   (end)

4. It's 9:00 a.m.

   The museum _____ .
   (open)

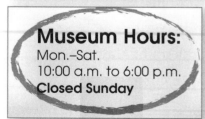

Check your answers. See page 135.

3 Max and Maria are planning a birthday party. Complete the sentences and answer the questions. Use the present perfect.

> **TO DO**
>
> **Max**
> bring my CDs ✓
> get a present
> buy drinks ✓
>
> **Maria**
> invite friends ✓
> bake a cake
>
> **Max and Maria**
> set up tables and chairs
> put up decorations ✓

1. __Has__ Max ____brought____ his CDs yet?   ____Yes, he has.____

2. _____ Maria _____ their friends yet?   _____

3. _____ Max _____ a present yet?   _____

4. _____ Maria _____ a cake yet?   _____

5. _____ Max _____ drinks yet?   _____

6. _____ Max and Maria _____ tables

   and chairs yet?   _____

7. _____ Max and Maria _____ decorations yet?   _____

4 Each of the sentences below is missing a word. Write the sentences with the missing word in parentheses.

1. We haven't gone to the park. (yet)

   __We haven't gone to the park yet.__

2. Our favorite TV show hasn't yet. (started)

   _____

3. Have bought tickets for the fund-raiser yet? (you)

   _____

4. They eaten lunch yet. (haven't)

   _____

5. Ivan and Alex already been to that restaurant. (have)

   _____

6. Julie visited the art exhibit yet? (has)

   _____

Check your answers. See page 135.

1 Read the sentences. Scan the article. Circle *T* (true) or *F* (false).

1. Four hundred people attended this superb performance.   T   (F)
2. The show started at 7:00 p.m. with Alvarez's band.   T   F
3. Alvarez performed four new songs.   T   F
4. Alvarez performed with three other musicians.   T   F
5. Alvarez played the guitar and maracas.   T   F
6. Some people waited in line for 30 minutes to buy a soda.   T   F
7. There was no food available after 9:00 p.m.   T   F
8. Alvarez performed until 11:00 p.m.   T   F
9. There will be three more performances at the Grand Theater.   T   F

RUDY ALVAREZ at the Park Theater

by Mike Clark

A huge crowd gathered to see the classical rock musician Rudy Alvarez perform at the Park Theater on Saturday night. Over 500 people attended this superb event.

The show started at 7:00 p.m. with a salsa band. The band's music was unremarkable, and the lead singer did not sing well at all. It was irritating, and everyone wanted Alvarez to come on stage. Finally, the salsa band finished, and Alvarez came on stage at 8:30 p.m. The versatile artist performed his most popular songs and five new songs. He played with three other musicians on guitars and drums. The audience went wild! Everyone danced and sang along, and children climbed onto the stage and started dancing.

One negative side to the event was that the lines were long for refreshments. Some people waited in line for 30 minutes to buy a soda, and there was no food available after 9:00 p.m. I also expected Alvarez to perform until about 11:00 p.m., but he ended the show at 10:30 p.m. because of excessive noise from the audience.

Alvarez will give three more performances at the Park Theater and one additional performance at the Grand Theater. If you haven't attended one of his shows yet, don't miss your chance!

Check your answers. See page 135.

2 Read the article in Exercise 1. Circle the answers.

1. Why did the concert finish early?
   a. The weather was bad.
   b. The lines were too long.
   c. The audience was too noisy.
   d. There were ominous black clouds.

2. What word did Mike Clark use to describe the salsa band?
   a. popular
   b. ominous
   c. excessive
   d. unremarkable

3. What word did Mike Clark use to describe Alvarez?
   a. superb
   b. versatile
   c. irritating
   d. ominous

4. Which statement is true?
   a. The audience liked the salsa band.
   b. The audience didn't make enough noise.
   c. Alvarez played his least popular songs.
   d. Alvarez played his most popular songs.

5. What was one negative thing about the concert?
   a. Children tried to get on stage.
   b. The concert finished too early.
   c. Alvarez's music was unremarkable.
   d. The musicians played guitars and drums.

3 Look at the bold words. Write the sentences. Use words from the box with a similar meaning.

crowd	excessive	missed	musicians	superb	unremarkable

1. We **didn't go** to the concert.   _We missed the concert._
2. The concert was **excellent**.   _____
3. There was a **large group of people**.   _____
4. The volume of the music was **too high**.   _____
5. There were five **people playing drums**.   _____
6. The stage was **not interesting**.   _____

Check your answers. See page 135.

1 Complete the word maps.

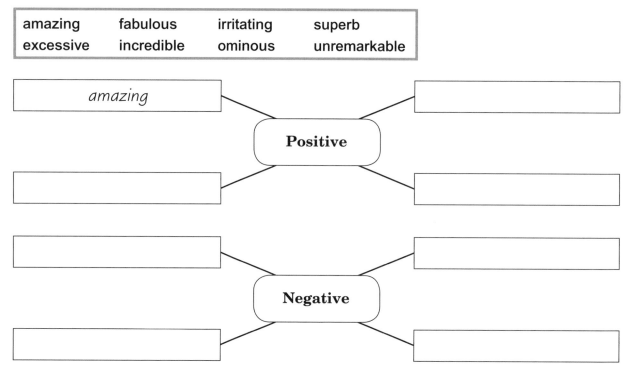

| amazing | fabulous | irritating | superb |
| excessive | incredible | ominous | unremarkable |

amazing

Positive

Negative

2 Read the postcard. Circle three positive adjectives. Underline three negative adjectives.

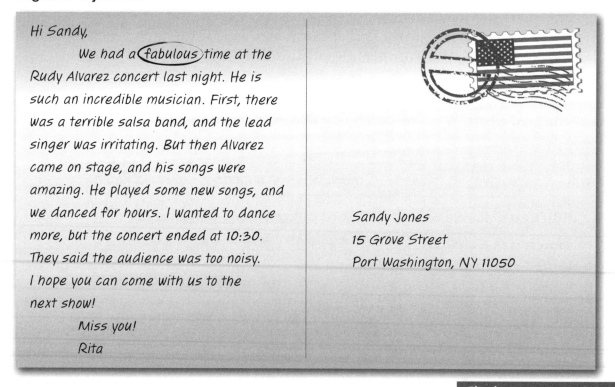

Hi Sandy,

We had a (fabulous) time at the Rudy Alvarez concert last night. He is such an incredible musician. First, there was a terrible salsa band, and the lead singer was irritating. But then Alvarez came on stage, and his songs were amazing. He played some new songs, and we danced for hours. I wanted to dance more, but the concert ended at 10:30. They said the audience was too noisy. I hope you can come with us to the next show!

Miss you!

Rita

Sandy Jones
15 Grove Street
Port Washington, NY 11050

Check your answers. See page 135.

3 Match the sentence parts. Write *N* for negative information and *P* for positive information.

1. <u>N</u> The musicians were irritating because
2. ____ Our seats were in the back, so
3. ____ The weather was bad, and
4. ____ The music was awesome, and
5. ____ The music wasn't loud enough, and

a. we couldn't see very well.
b. they couldn't sing.
c. we danced all night.
d. we couldn't hear anything.
e. we were cold.

4 Read Bill's notes about a jazz concert. Write an e-mail about the concert. Use positive and negative information.

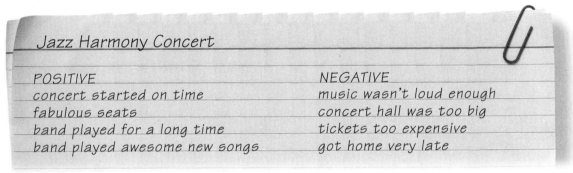

Jazz Harmony Concert

POSITIVE	NEGATIVE
concert started on time	music wasn't loud enough
fabulous seats	concert hall was too big
band played for a long time	tickets too expensive
band played awesome new songs	got home very late

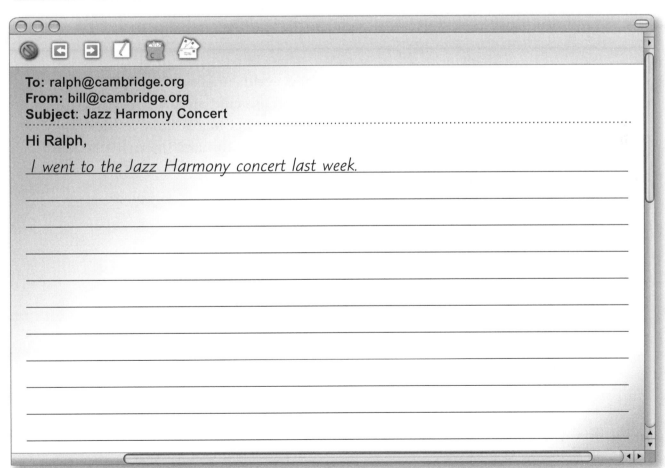

To: ralph@cambridge.org
From: bill@cambridge.org
Subject: Jazz Harmony Concert

Hi Ralph,

I went to the Jazz Harmony concert last week.

Check your answers. See page 135.

Another view

1 Read the questions. Look at the announcements. Circle the answers.

INTERNATIONAL FAIR

Food and music from twenty different countries. Sat. 10:00 a.m. to 5:00 p.m., Sun. 10:00 a.m. to 3:00 p.m. at the Community Center. Free admission.

WILDLIFE MOVIES

Educational films – fun for children and adults. Wednesday, September 19th, at 5:00 p.m. East Riverside Public Library. No admission fee.

NATURE TOUR

Have you joined the Friends of Mission Park yet? Come for an easy guided walk around the park on Sunday. Meet at the Information Center at noon. Tickets: $3.00 for adults, $2.00 for children.

COMMUNITY BARBECUE

Have you seen your friends and neighbors lately? Then join us for burgers and all the fixin's. This Sunday, 11:00 to 3:00. All you can eat meal tickets: $7.00.

1. At which event can you get some exercise?
   a. Nature Tour
   b. Wildlife Movies
   c. International Fair
   d. Community Barbecue

2. Which event starts at 10:00 a.m. on Sunday?
   a. Nature Tour
   b. Wildlife Movies
   c. International Fair
   d. Community Barbecue

3. Which event is the most expensive?
   a. Nature Tour
   b. Wildlife Movies
   c. International Fair
   d. Community Barbecue

4. Which events are free?
   a. International Fair and Nature Tour
   b. Nature Tour and Wildlife Movies
   c. Wildlife Movies and International Fair
   d. Community Barbecue and Nature Tour

5. Which event does not take place on a weekend?
   a. Nature Tour
   b. Wildlife Movies
   c. International Fair
   d. Community Barbecue

6. At which events can you eat food?
   a. Community Barbecue and Nature Tour
   b. Wildlife Movies and Community Barbecue
   c. International Fair and Nature Tour
   d. Community Barbecue and International Fair

Check your answers. See page 135.

2 Circle the correct word.

1. Sue is going to see an art exhibit at the **theater** / **museum** / **restaurant**.

2. Chandra plans to go to an outdoor concert in the **restaurant** / **park** / **library**.

3. Maurice would like to take a walking tour around the **gym** / **gardens** / **restaurant**.

4. Hakim wants to have a picnic in the **library** / **museum** / **park**.

5. Nu wants to watch travel movies at the **library** / **gym** / **restaurant**.

6. Esme hopes to take dance classes at the **museum** / **restaurant** / **gym**.

3 Check (✓). Where can you do these activities?

	Park only	Park and library	Library only
ride a bike	✓		
see a movie			
borrow a book			
play baseball			
meet friends			
play the guitar			
listen to music			
go jogging			
play cards			
eat ice cream			
read magazines			
have lunch			
study			
socialize			
take a walk			
be alone			

Check your answers. See page 135.

Lesson A *Get ready*

Time

1 Complete Olivia's journal entry.

| chores | due | impatient | prioritize | procrastinating | to-do list |

I have too many things to do today. My friends are coming over for dinner tonight. I need to make a ___to-do list___ and stop _____ . I have to buy food for
　　　　　　　　　　　　　1　　　　　　　　　　　　　　　　2

dinner. I have some _____ to do around the house, and I also have to finish
　　　　　　　　　　　　　3

my homework. It's _____ tomorrow. Now I need to _____ the
　　　　　　　　　　　　4　　　　　　　　　　　　　　　　　　　　5

tasks on my list. First, I want to do the shopping because it is the most important. Next, I'll

cook the food. My friends might get _____ if they have to wait for dinner.
　　　　　　　　　　　　　　　　　　　　6

Then, I'll clean up the house. Will I have time to do my homework before they arrive?

Probably not.

2 Circle the answers. Use the information in Exercise 1.

1. What is Olivia's problem?
   a. She has too many things to do.
   b. She has too much homework.
   c. She doesn't want to prioritize.
   d. She doesn't have enough work to do.

2. Olivia needs to stop _____ .
   a. cooking
   b. procrastinating
   c. doing chores
   d. doing her homework

3. What will she do before she cooks?
   a. clean up
   b. go shopping
   c. take out the trash
   d. finish her homework

4. When Olivia *prioritizes*, she'll do _____ .
   a. some of her tasks
   b. the most difficult tasks later
   c. the most important tasks first
   d. all of the tasks as quickly as possible

5. When friends are *impatient*, they are not willing to _____ .
   a. eat
   b. wait
   c. prioritize
   d. procrastinate

6. When you don't *have time*, you are too _____ .
   a. busy
   b. late
   c. upset
   d. tired

Check your answers. See page 135.

3 Number Olivia's tasks in the order she plans to do them. Use the information in Exercise 1.

Olivia's to-do list

____ do homework

____ clean up the house

____ spend time with friends

____ cook the food

_1_ buy food

4 Complete the sentences.

chores	due	prioritize	tasks
deadline	impatient	procrastinating	

1. I have to do some _____*chores*_____ and take out the trash.

2. The _____ for my project is tomorrow.

3. I have another project _____ next week.

4. You have to make a to-do list of _____ in order of importance.

5. Do your homework now and stop _____ !

6. I have too many things to do this weekend. I need to

_____ them.

7. Please don't be so _____ ! Your food will be ready soon.

5 Match.

1. do _b_   a. impatient
2. make ____   b. homework
3. take out ____   c. tasks
4. prioritize ____ d. the trash
5. be ____   e. a to-do list

Check your answers. See page 135.

Dependent clauses

Study the explanation on page 129.

1 Make sentences. Match the sentence parts.

1. When I need to concentrate, _b_
2. When I feel tired, ____
3. When I have a deadline, ____
4. When I don't understand a grammar question, ____
5. When I don't understand a word, ____
6. When I have many tasks to do, ____

a. I don't answer the phone.
b. I turn off the TV.
c. I use a dictionary.
d. I make a to-do list.
e. I drink some coffee.
f. I ask my teacher.

2 Combine the sentences. Use *when*.

1. Parvana has a lot of homework. She makes a list of her tasks.

   When _Parvana has a lot of homework, she makes a list of her tasks_ .

2. She wants to concentrate. She goes to the library.

   When _____ , _____ .

3. She looks at the clock. She starts her work.

   _____ when _____ .

4. She finishes a task. She checks it off her list.

   When _____ , _____ .

5. She takes a short break. She feels tired.

   _____ when _____ .

6. She doesn't hand in her homework on time. Her teacher is upset.

   When _____ , _____ .

7. She eats a snack. She feels hungry.

   _____ when _____ .

8. She needs to focus. She doesn't answer the phone.

   When _____ , _____ .

9. She does the difficult tasks first. She has a lot of work to do.

   _____ when _____ .

10. She has a deadline. She doesn't procrastinate.

    When _____ , _____ .

Check your answers. See page 135.

3 Read the sentences. Add commas if necessary. Write *no comma* if you do not need a comma.

1. When I finish my homework, I take a break. _____

2. Than procrastinates when he doesn't want to do his homework. _____

3. Suzanna uses a dictionary when she reads the newspaper. _____

4. When we don't hand in our homework our teacher is very upset. _____

5. When I have a deadline I stay up late. _____

6. Sushila doesn't like to work when she is tired. _____

4 Write questions. Then write the answers.

I ask my teacher.	I procrastinate.	I study my notes.
I go to the library.	I rest.	I take a break.

1. (do / finish a difficult task)

   A What *do you do when you finish a difficult task* ?

   B *I take a break* .

2. (do / need to concentrate)

   A What _____ ?

   B _____ .

3. (do / don't understand the homework)

   A What _____ ?

   B _____ .

4. (do / have a quiz or test)

   A What _____ ?

   B _____ .

5. (do / feel tired)

   A What _____ ?

   B _____ .

6. (do / have a deadline)

   A What _____ ?

   B _____ .

Check your answers. See page 136.

Lesson C Dependent clauses

Study the explanation on page 129.

1 Complete the sentences. Use *after*.

Mannie's morning schedule

5:30 wake up
5:45 get dressed
6:00 eat breakfast
6:30 work out
7:15 take a shower
8:00 go to work

1. Mannie gets dressed _____ *after he wakes up* _____ .

2. Mannie eats breakfast _____ .

3. Mannie works out _____ .

4. Mannie takes a shower _____ .

5. Mannie goes to work _____ .

2 Write sentences. Use *before*.

Mannie's evening schedule

5:30 get home
6:00 eat dinner
7:00 do homework
8:00 watch TV
9:00 read a book
9:30 go to sleep

1. get home / eat dinner

   Mannie gets home before he eats dinner. _____

2. eat dinner / do homework

   _____

3. do homework / watch TV

   _____

4. watch TV / read a book

   _____

Check your answers. See page 136.

3 Write questions. Answer the questions. Use the information in Exercises 1 and 2.

1. Mannie / do / before / eat breakfast

   A What _does Mannie do before he eats breakfast_ ?

   B _He gets dressed._

2. Mannie / do / before / work out

   A What _____ ?

   B _____

3. Mannie / do / before / go to work

   A What _____ ?

   B _____

4. Mannie / do / after / get home

   A What _____ ?

   B _____

5. Mannie / do / after / watch TV

   A What _____ ?

   B _____

6. Mannie / do / after / read a book

   A What _____ ?

   B _____

4 Underline the activity that happens first. Circle the activity that happens second.

1. (I watch TV) after I have dinner.

2. Before Sandy goes to work, she buys a newspaper.

3. Ivana goes to school after she finishes work.

4. After Simon finishes his homework, he takes a break.

5. They usually go swimming after they go to the park.

6. Before you go out, you need to take out the trash.

7. Melanie puts on makeup after she takes a shower.

8. Alan washes the dishes before he goes to bed.

Check your answers. See page 136.

Reading

1 Read the article. Circle the answers.

Personal Rules about Time

Everyone has his or her own personal rules about time. These rules depend on the personality of the person as well as on the culture of the country.

Some individuals – no matter where they are from – have very strict rules about time. They like to keep a schedule. They are always early for meetings. When they catch a train, they arrive at the station 30 minutes before the train leaves. When they go to a party, they are often the first guests to arrive. It is sometimes difficult for these people to understand why their co-workers and friends cannot be on time. They get angry when their friends are late.

Other people are not very strict about time – even in places like the United States, Canada, and England, where punctuality is generally considered to be very important. They don't think keeping a schedule is the most important thing. For example, they are sometimes late for work, they often miss trains and buses, and they arrive at a party one or two hours after the party has started. They don't understand why other people get upset when they are late. On the other hand, these people do not get impatient when their friends are late!

1. This article talks about two different _____ .
   a. how to keep a schedule
   b. why punctuality is important
   c. ways of thinking about time
   d. types of social and business events

2. When people are strict about time, they _____ .
   a. keep a schedule
   b. come from special countries
   c. are always late for appointments
   d. are good and understanding friends

3. When people are not strict about time, they are _____ .
   a. never late
   b. not punctual
   c. schedule keepers
   d. always impatient

4. According to the article, you should _____ .
   a. always be on time
   b. have personal rules about time
   c. understand your friends
   d. understand different rules about time

Check your answers. See page 136.

2 Complete the sentences.

impatient	impolite	irresponsible	punctuality	uncommon

1. In Canada, it is _____*impolite*_____ to arrive at a dinner party more than ten minutes late.

2. People who are strict about time get _____ when their friends are late.

3. In England, _____ is an unspoken rule. Being on time is important.

4. It is _____ to be late for a job interview in the United States.

5. In Brazil, it is not _____ for guests to arrive two hours after a social event begins.

3 Rewrite the sentences. Write the **bold** words with the prefixes *un-*, *dis-*, *ir-*, or *im-*.

1. It is **not common** to miss a plane.

   It is uncommon to miss a plane.

2. It is **not polite** to be late.

   _____

3. It is **not usual** to be early for a party.

   _____

4. He is **not patient**.

   _____

5. They are **not responsible**.

   _____

6. She is **not organized**.

   _____

4 Write the opposites.

1. unlucky _____*lucky*_____
2. impossible _____
3. dishonest _____
4. unfriendly _____
5. unkind _____
6. irrational _____

Check your answers. See page 136.

Writing

1 Read the paragraph. Answer the questions.

An Organized Student

Nita is a very organized person. For example, she keeps all of her class notes in one binder with different sections. Each section has a label. She also writes all of her homework assignments and due dates in a special notebook. Before she goes home, she checks her bag carefully. She makes sure she has all the books she needs. After she gets home, she has dinner. Then she plans how much time she will need for each assignment. She makes a list of tasks and crosses them out when she finishes them. When she feels tired, she takes a short break. In summary, Nita is an organized person and a successful student.

---

1. What is the topic sentence?

   Nita is a very organized person.

2. What is the first example?

   _____

3. What is the second example?

   _____

4. Which words signal the conclusion?

   _____

2 Answer the questions. Use the information in Exercise 1.

1. Why doesn't Nita forget the due dates of her assignments?

   She writes all her homework assignments and the due dates in a special notebook.

2. Where does she keep her notes?

   _____

3. What does she do before she goes home?

   _____

4. What does she plan after dinner?

   _____

5. What does she do when she feels tired?

   _____

Check your answers. See page 136.

3 Write the sentences in the correct order to make a paragraph.

> ## An Impatient Boss
>
> She is also not a good listener, and she often interrupts.
> For example, she often gets angry when you are three minutes late.
> Finally, she is always in a hurry and never has enough time.
> My boss Frida is a very impatient person.
> In conclusion, Frida is a very impatient person, and it is difficult to work for her.

My boss Frida is a very impatient person.
_____
_____
_____
_____
_____

4 Write a short paragraph about Paula. Include a topic sentence, examples to support your topic sentence, and a signal before your conclusion.

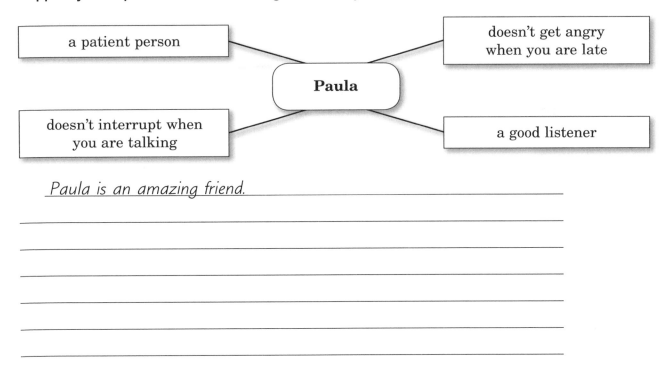

Paula is an amazing friend.
_____
_____
_____
_____
_____
_____

Check your answers. See page 136.

1 Read the questions. Look at the pie chart. Circle the answers.

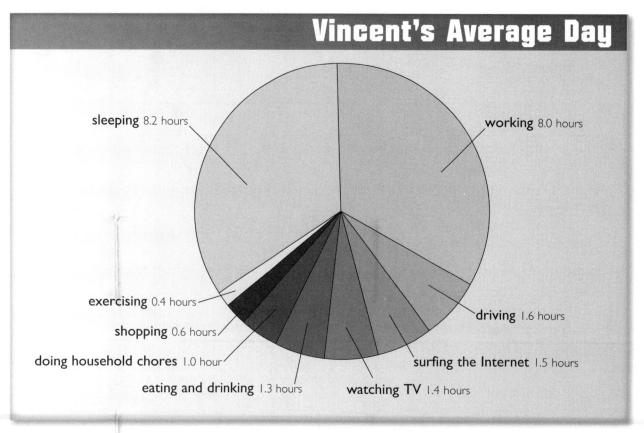

Vincent's Average Day

sleeping 8.2 hours

working 8.0 hours

exercising 0.4 hours

shopping 0.6 hours

doing household chores 1.0 hour

eating and drinking 1.3 hours

watching TV 1.4 hours

surfing the Internet 1.5 hours

driving 1.6 hours

1. Which activity does Vincent spend the most time doing?
   a. driving
   b. working
   c. sleeping
   d. watching TV

2. Which activity does Vincent spend the least time doing?
   a. eating
   b. driving
   c. shopping
   d. exercising

3. How much time does Vincent spend doing household chores?
   a. 0.4 hours
   b. 0.6 hours
   c. 1.0 hour
   d. 1.3 hours

4. Vincent spends more time _____ .
   a. working than sleeping
   b. watching TV than eating and drinking
   c. shopping than doing household chores
   d. doing household chores than eating and drinking

5. Vincent spends as much time _____ .
   a. shopping and exercising as doing household chores
   b. eating and drinking as doing household chores and exercising
   c. driving as watching TV and exercising
   d. surfing the Internet as exercising and shopping

Check your answers. See page 137.

2 Complete the sentences.

in time	on time	save time	spend time	take your time	waste time

1. You shouldn't _____*waste time*_____ watching so much TV.

2. Joe never takes the stairs at work. He takes the elevator to _____ .

3. She didn't leave her house _____ to catch the train.

4. We always start meetings _____ .

5. There's no need to hurry. You can _____ .

6. I don't _____ cooking. I usually eat out.

3 Read about the students. Answer the questions.

Hiroshi

I usually get to the concert at least half an hour before it starts.

Carla

Where are my keys? Oh, no! They're in my jacket. Where's my jacket?

Phil

My manager says that I interrupt people when they're talking.

Benita

Hurry! We don't want to be late!

Paco

I have so much homework to do. But first I need to have some coffee, and then I want to watch TV.

Adela

OK, we'll start at 2:00 p.m. We'll work until 4:00 and then take a ten-minute break.

1. Who is disorganized? ___*Carla*___   4. Who is impatient? _____

2. Who is punctual? _____   5. Who likes to keep a schedule? _____

3. Who procrastinates? _____   6. Who is impolite? _____

Check your answers. See page 137.

Shopping

1 Read the conversation. Circle the answers.

Sofia Do you use your credit card a lot?

Jackie Yes. All the time! I have four cards.

Sofia Really? Isn't it difficult to pay them off? The interest rates are so high!

Jackie I never charge more than $100 on each card.

Sofia I'm thinking about buying a new refrigerator, but I can't afford it.

Jackie Why don't you buy it on credit? You can pay for it later.

Sofia I don't want to get into debt. We already have to pay off our car loan.

Jackie Maybe you could look in the newspaper and find a used refrigerator.

Sofia That's a good idea.

1. Sofia wants to buy a refrigerator. What is the problem?

   a. She doesn't have a car.

   b. She doesn't have any credit.

   c. She doesn't have a credit card.

   d. She doesn't have enough money.

2. What does Jackie think Sofia should do?

   a. take out a loan

   b. get a new credit card

   c. pay off her car loan

   d. buy a used refrigerator

3. Which statement is true?

   a. Sofia wants a new credit card.

   b. Sofia never borrows money.

   c. Sofia is worried about getting into debt.

   d. Sofia needs to borrow money for her car loan.

4. Which statement is true?

   a. Jackie never uses a credit card.

   b. Jackie has more than one credit card.

   c. Jackie uses her credit card every day.

   d. Jackie spends too much on her credit card.

Check your answers. See page 137.

2 Complete the sentences.

| afford | balance | cash | cost | on credit | used |

1. I don't have enough money for that car. I can't _____ *afford* _____ it.

2. I am going to use my credit card. I'll buy this refrigerator _____ and pay later.

3. I don't want to get into debt. I always pay _____ for everything.

4. The interest rate is high. It will _____ a lot of money.

5. We don't have much money in the bank. Our account _____ is low.

6. I'm not going to buy a new car. I'm going to buy a _____ one.

3 Solve the problems.

1. Su Lin and Chung Hee have a balance of $28,000.00 in their savings account. They want to buy a new car that costs $30,500.00. If they use all the money in their savings account, how much do they need to borrow to buy the new car? _____ *$2,500.00* _____

   Cost of new car: $30,500.00
   Balance in savings account: -$28,000.00
   Money they need to borrow: $2,500.00

2. Suzanne and Pete have a balance of $950.00 in their savings account. They want to buy a new refrigerator. It costs $1,200.00. If they use all the money in their savings account, how much do they need to borrow to buy the refrigerator? _____

3. Dora and Julian have a balance of $1,500.00 in their savings account. They want to buy a new television. It costs $1,200.00. They also need a new washing machine. It costs $800.00. If they use all the money in their savings account, how much do they need to borrow to buy the TV and the washing machine? _____

Check your answers. See page 137.

Lesson B Modals

Study the chart on page 126.

1 Match the problems with the suggestions.

1. I can't afford gas for my car. __*b*__
2. My credit card bills are too high. ____
3. I need to find a job. ____
4. I can't afford a new winter coat. ____
5. My rent is too expensive. ____
6. My cell phone bill is too high. ____

a. You could use e-mail instead.
b. You could take the bus.
c. You could find a cheaper apartment.
d. You could look at help-wanted ads.
e. You could talk to a debt counselor.
f. You could use your credit card.

2 Circle the correct form of the verb.

1. You should (buy)/ **buying** a new car.
2. How about **take** / **taking** out a loan?
3. You could **use** / **using** a credit card.
4. Why don't you **talk** / **talking** to a debt counselor?
5. You should **apply** / **applying** for a scholarship.
6. How about **look** / **looking** in the newspaper?

3 Complete the sentences. Use *could* or *should*.

1. *A* I don't have enough money at the end of each month.
   Do you have any advice?

   B You ___*should*___ try to save a little each month.

2. *A* Where do you suggest I buy a new camera?

   B You _____ find one online, or you could go to the mall.

3. *A* I don't know how to apply for college. Can you give me any advice?

   B You _____ talk to a counselor.

4. *A* My tooth hurts. What should I do?

   B You _____ go to the dentist.

5. *A* Can you suggest a good place to go on vacation?

   B You _____ go to Hawaii, or why don't you go to Las Vegas?

6. *A* I want to get a good grade on my test. What should I do?

   B You _____ study hard this weekend.

Check your answers. See page 137.

4 Complete the sentences.

ask the store to send a repair person	put some in the freezer
asking her what she wants	sell it
buying a book about computers	take them back to the store

1. **A** I bought these shoes yesterday, but I don't like them. What should I do?

   B You should _take them back to the store_ .

2. **A** I bought a new refrigerator, but it doesn't work. Do you have any suggestions?

   B You could _____ .

3. **A** I bought a new computer, but I don't know how to use it.

   B How about _____ ?

4. **A** I bought too much food at the supermarket.

   B Why don't you _____ ?

5. **A** I bought a new car, but I can't afford the payments. What should I do?

   B You should _____ .

6. **A** I bought a present for my girlfriend, but she doesn't like it.

   B How about _____ ?

5 Complete the sentences. Use *should* and the verbs in the box.

buy	do	make	tell	wear

1. **A** We don't have plans this weekend. What _____ *should we do* _____ ?

   B I don't know. Maybe we could go to the movies.

2. **A** I didn't finish the homework. What _____ my teacher?

   B You should tell your teacher the truth. You didn't have enough time.

3. **A** I'm going shopping tomorrow. What _____ ?

   B I think you should get a new pair of pants.

4. **A** I want to make a special dinner tonight. What _____ ?

   B Well, I like fish.

5. **A** I don't have any nice clothes for the party. What _____ ?

   B You should borrow my black jacket.

Check your answers. See page 137.

Lesson C *Gerunds*

Study the chart and explanation on page 122.

1 Write the gerund form of each verb.

1. apply *applying*
2. be _____
3. buy _____
4. find _____

5. get _____
6. lend _____
7. lose _____
8. make _____

9. open _____
10. pay _____
11. study _____
12. wait _____

2 Complete the sentences. Use words in Exercise 1.

1. He is tired of *waiting* .
2. She is happy about _____ a new car.
3. He is interested in _____ for a loan.
4. She is thinking about _____ a savings account.
5. He is excited about _____ auto mechanics.
6. She is afraid of _____ into debt.

Check your answers. See page 137.

3 Circle the correct preposition.

1. Martina is worried (about) / of paying her bills.

2. Sam is happy **about** / **of** starting college next week.

3. Tran is tired **about** / **of** working in a supermarket.

4. Louisa is thinking **about** / **in** going to school next semester.

5. I want to thank you **about** / **for** helping me.

4 Complete the sentences.

about finding a job	for driving me to work	of getting up early
about getting a scholarship	in learning about computers	of losing their jobs

1. I'm worried _about finding a job_ .

2. Thank you _____ .

3. Serena is happy _____ .

4. Chang is tired _____ .

5. Lisa and Theo are afraid _____ .

6. Maurice is interested _____ .

5 Complete the sentences. Use the information in the chart.

Name	Feelings	Activity
Ron	excited	go to college
Miguel	afraid	lose his job
Vincent and Anna	happy	pay off their loan
Tim and Betsy	worried	get into debt
Steve	interested	buy a new car
Isabella	tired	get home late every day

1. Ron _is excited about going to college_ .

2. Miguel _____ .

3. Vincent and Anna _____ .

4. Tim and Betsy _____ .

5. Steve _____ .

6. Isabella _____ .

Check your answers. See page 137.

1 Read the article. Answer the questions.

How many credit cards should you have?

How many credit cards do you have in your wallet? Are you worried about getting into debt? Many Americans carry four or five credit cards, but others have more than ten. Is it a good idea to have so many credit cards?

Some people almost never pay cash. It's easier to use a credit card. They use their credit cards for everything – food, clothes, gas, utility bills, and rent. However, when the bills arrive, people who have too many cards sometimes can't afford the minimum payments. It's also difficult to keep track of so many cards.

It's not uncommon to have store credit cards. Some stores offer a 10–15 percent discount when you use their credit card. They also offer coupons and other discounts. But be careful. The interest rates on these cards can be very high. It's a good idea to use a store credit card at your favorite store if you shop there often. But you should pay off the account balance immediately. That way, you won't pay any interest.

Debt counselors say that it's a good idea to have at least two cards. Use one card for everyday living expenses, and keep the other one for emergencies. They suggest choosing credit cards with low interest rates, keeping your account balance low, always trying to pay more than just the minimum payments, and having no more than six cards.

1. What happens to some people when they have too many credit cards?
   They can't afford the minimum payments.

2. What do some stores offer when you use their credit card?
   _____

3. Why is it important to pay off your account balance immediately?
   _____

4. How many credit cards do debt counselors say you should have?
   _____

> *Check your answers. See page 137.*

2 Write four tips for using credit cards. Use the information from the article in Exercise 1.

1. *Choose credit cards with low interest rates.* _____
2. _____
3. _____
4. _____

3 Match.

1. minimum *e*   a. card
2. credit ____   b. budget
3. interest ____   c. counselor
4. debt ____   d. rate
5. family ____   e. payment

4 Complete the sentences. Use words in Exercise 3.

1. I don't have any _____*credit*_____ cards.
2. The _____ rate is very high.
3. We always make a family _____ .
4. What is the _____ payment?
5. Why don't you talk to a debt _____ ?

5 Complete the sentences. Use words in Exercise 3.

1. I canceled my credit card because the _____*interest rate*_____ was over 25 percent.
2. We made a _____ . Now we can save enough every month.
3. When you use a _____ , you borrow money and pay it back later.
4. We talked to a _____ to help us solve our financial problems.
5. The smallest payment you can make each month is the _____ .

Check your answers. See page 137.

Writing

1 Match the money problems with the suggestions.

1. I don't have enough money to buy lunch. __c__
2. I'm worried about being in debt. _____
3. I don't have enough nice clothes for work. _____
4. I'm too tired to cook dinner after work, but take-out meals are unhealthy. _____

a. Why don't you cook meals on the weekends and freeze them?
b. You could go to a thrift store.
c. How about bringing lunch from home?
d. You should see a debt counselor.

2 Read the letters. Answer the questions.

Dear Money Guy,

I drive to work every day, but gas is very expensive. My car uses a lot of gas, and I can't afford to fill up my car. I also need to see an auto mechanic for repairs. I am worried about having the car break down on the way to work. What should I do? Can you give me advice?

Worried Larry

Dear Worried Larry,

I have a few suggestions for you. First, ask a co-worker to give you a ride to work, and you can share the cost of gas. Second, you could drive to work three times a week and take the bus twice a week. Finally, you could think about taking the bus for a couple of months and saving money for your car repairs. You might enjoy taking the bus. Then you could sell your car!

Money Guy

1. What are Worried Larry's problems?

    a. *Gas is very expensive.* _____

    b. _____

    c. _____

    d. _____

2. What are Money Guy's suggestions?

    a. _____

    b. _____

    c. _____

Check your answers. See page 137.

3 Read the letter to Money Guy.

Dear Money Guy,

    I spend too much money on clothes. I don't really need new clothes, but when I go to the mall, I always want to buy something new. I use my store credit card. At first, I tried to pay off my bill every month. But now I have reached my spending limit, and the bills are too high. What should I do?

Clothes Crazy

4 Read the solutions. Write an answer to Clothes Crazy. Give Clothes Crazy some suggestions. Use *First*, *Second*, *Third*, and *Finally*.

Solution 1	Solution 2	Solution 3	Solution 4
Pay all your bills before you go back to the mall.	After you pay your bills, cancel your store credit card. Always pay cash.	Make a list of clothes you really need before you go shopping.	Go shopping with a friend. Ask your friend's advice before you buy anything.

Dear Clothes Crazy,

    I have a few suggestions for you. _____

_____

_____

_____

_____

_____

_____

_____

_____

_____

_____

I hope this advice is helpful!

Money Guy

Check your answers. See page 137.

Another view

1 Read the questions. Look at the credit card brochure. Circle the answers.

	City Spender credit card	Super Express credit card
Annual fee	• none	• 1st year free, then $75
Monthly interest rate	• 0% interest rate for the first six months • After six months, the interest rate is 13.4%	• 0% interest rate for the first three months • After three months, the interest rate is 11.49%
Rewards program	• Five points for every $1.00 spent	• One point for every $1.00 spent • 1,000 bonus points with your first purchase and 100 bonus points with your 100th purchase
Minimum monthly payment	• 1% of the account balance	• 2% of the account balance

1. What is the interest rate with a Super Express credit card after two months?
   a. 0%
   b. 1%
   c. 2%
   d. 11.49%

2. What does the City Spender credit card offer?
   a. bonus points with the first purchase
   b. one reward point for every $5.00 spent
   c. 0% interest for the first six months
   d. 13.4% interest for the first three months

3. What does the Super Express credit card offer?
   a. 0% interest for the first 6 months
   b. one reward point for every dollar spent
   c. no annual fee in the second year
   d. none of the above

4. What is the minimum monthly payment with a City Spender credit card?
   a. 0% of the account balance
   b. 1% of the account balance
   c. 2% of the account balance
   d. 13.4% of the account balance

5. Which is true about both credit cards?
   a. no annual fees in the first year
   b. 2% minimum monthly payment
   c. 0% interest for the first six months
   d. all of the above

6. Which is true about both credit cards?
   a. one point for every dollar spent
   b. 11.49% interest for the first three months
   c. both *a* and *b*
   d. neither *a* nor *b*

Check your answers. See page 138.

2 Read the chart. Answer the questions.

How do you like to spend your money?

	Jewelry	Clothes	Movies	Eating out	Gifts	CDs and books
Jerry				✓	✓	✓
Anya	✓	✓	✓			
Klara		✓			✓	
Luis	✓		✓	✓		✓

1. Who likes spending money on clothes and gifts? _____Klara_____

2. Who likes spending money on jewelry and clothes? _____

3. Who likes spending money on CDs and books but not on gifts? _____

4. Who likes spending money on jewelry but not on clothes? _____

5. Who doesn't like spending money on clothes and movies? _____

6. Who doesn't like spending money on eating out and movies? _____

3 Complete the puzzle.

account	cash	credit	debt	interest	thrift

Across

1. I don't have a credit card. I pay _____ .

5. When you borrow money, you must pay _____ .

6. I don't buy new clothes. I go to the _____ store.

Down

2. You can keep your money in a bank _____ .

3. If you don't pay your bills, you'll get into _____ .

4. You can use your _____ card to buy something now and pay for it later.

Check your answers. See page 138.

Work

1 Complete the paragraph.

| college | degree | employed | gets along | personnel | shift | strengths |

Marina is from Senegal and has been living in the United States for one year. She has been _____employed_____ as a cashier in a drugstore for about
1

six months. Her _____ are that she is responsible and friendly.
2

She _____ well with her co-workers. Three nights a week, she
3

goes to _____ . She is taking business courses at night and
4

wants to get a _____ in hotel management.
5

Last week, she applied for a job as a reservations clerk at a big hotel. In the future, she hopes to get a job as an assistant manager or a manager. Today she got a call from the _____ manager asking her to
6

come in for an interview.

Marina is confident that she can do the job. She speaks English well, and she speaks French fluently. She knows how to use a computer, a copy machine, and a fax machine. But she can't work the night

_____ because of her business classes.
7

2 Complete the chart. Use the information about Marina in Exercise 1.

Topic	Marina's answers
1. job she is applying for	*reservations clerk*
2. native country	
3. current job	
4. office machines she can use	
5. strengths	

Check your answers. See page 138.

3 Answer the personnel manager's questions. Use the information about Marina in Exercise 1.

1. **A** Where are you from?

   B *I'm from Senegal.*

2. **A** Are you currently employed?

   B _____

3. **A** What kind of work do you do?

   B _____

4. **A** What office machines can you use?

   B _____

5. **A** What other job skills do you have?

   B _____

6. **A** Are you taking any classes to improve your job skills?

   B _____

7. **A** What are your personal strengths?

   B _____

8. **A** Can you work the night shift?

   B _____

4 Complete the sentences.

background	employed	interview	shift
degree	get along	personnel	strengths

1. I have many friends at school. I ____*get along*____ with everybody.

2. I'm going to college to get a _____ in accounting.

3. I don't have a job now. I am not currently _____ .

4. I sent my job application to the _____ manager.

5. One of my _____ is that I am very reliable.

6. I have a job _____ next week.

7. I can't work during the day. I need to work the night _____ .

8. Can you tell me more about your _____ ? I'd like to know more about you.

Check your answers. See page 138.

Present perfect continuous

Study the chart and explanation on page 125.

1 Complete the chart.

a long time	morning	September	Tuesday	2005	week
day	one hour	three months	2:00 p.m.	two weeks	year

for	since	all
a long time		

2 Write sentences. Use the present perfect continuous with *for*, *since*, and *all*.

1. Kendra / work / in the library / October

   Kendra has been working in the library since October.

2. Frank and Marta / study computers / two years

   _____

3. Carla / look for jobs / January

   _____

4. I / wait for an interview / 1:30 p.m.

   _____

5. You / talk on the phone / one hour

   _____

6. We / use the library computers / morning

   _____

7. Kemal / drive a cab / 20 years

   _____

8. Gloria / cook food / day

   _____

Check your answers. See page 138.

3 Write questions and two answers. Use the present perfect continuous with *for* and *since*.

1. Alicia and Claire started painting the house at 11:00 a.m. It is now 11:30 a.m.

   A How long _have Alicia and Claire been painting the house_ ?

   B Since _11:00 a.m._ .

   For _30 minutes_ .

2. Inez started cooking at 4:00 p.m. It is now 6:00 p.m.

   A How long _____ ?

   B Since _____ .

   For _____ .

3. Tony and Leon started studying computers on June 1st. Today is July 1st.

   A How long _____ ?

   B Since _____ .

   For _____ .

4. Yoshi started working in the hotel on Tuesday – five days ago.

   A How long _____ ?

   B Since _____ .

   For _____ .

5. I started using a computer in August. It is now November.

   A How long _____ ?

   B Since _____ .

   For _____ .

6. Lenka started driving this morning at 10:00 a.m. It is now 1:00 p.m.

   A How long _____ ?

   B Since _____ .

   For _____ .

7. Juan started attending this school three weeks ago. It is now February 5th.

   A How long _____ ?

   B Since _____ .

   For _____ .

Check your answers. See page 138.

Lesson C *Phrasal verbs*

Study the explanation and list of phrasal verbs on page 128.

1 Complete the sentences.

away	back	down	out	up

1. I'm busy now. Could you please call ____*back*____ later?

2. Could you please fill _____ this application?

3. I don't want to listen to music. Could you turn _____ the volume?

4. Could you clean _____ your room, please?

5. Please put _____ your dictionary. You can't use a dictionary during the test.

2 Look at the words in bold. Write the sentences again with *him*, *it*, or *them*.

1. Anton needs to turn down **the music**.

   He _*needs to turn it down*_____ .

2. Rita is cleaning up **the kitchen**.

   She _____ .

3. Martine is throwing away **old newspapers**.

   She _____ .

4. The students are putting away **their books**.

   They _____ .

5. I need to call back **my father**.

   I _____ .

6. You should turn off **the heat**.

   You _____ .

3 Complete the sentences. Use phrasal verbs and *him*, *it*, or *them*.

1. These clothes are clean. Please put _____*them away*_____ .

2. Your room is a mess! Please clean _____ .

3. Your husband just called and left a message. Please call _____ .

4. The volume on your cell phone is not loud enough. Please turn _____ .

5. Here is the job application. Please fill _____ .

Check your answers. See page 138.

4 Add the missing word in each sentence.

1. I don't have time to call ^him back. (him)

2. There's too much trash. Please throw out. (it)

3. We don't need these winter jackets anymore. Please put them. (away)

4. I want to watch TV. Let's turn on. (it)

5 Complete the sentences.

| call back | clean up | hand out | put away |

She's ___*putting away*___ her clothes.

She's ___*putting*___ her clothes ___*away*___ .

She's ___*putting*___ them ___*away*___ .

He's _____ the tests.

He's _____ the tests _____ .

He's _____ them _____ .

She's _____ her kitchen.

She's _____ her kitchen _____ .

She's _____ it _____ .

He's _____ Doctor Kim.

He's _____ Doctor Kim _____ .

He's _____ him _____ .

Check your answers. See page 138.

1 Scan the blog. Answer the questions.

1. Who wrote the blog?

   Ivan wrote the blog.

2. What is the blog about?

3. How long has the writer been writing the blog?

4. What does the writer ask readers to do?

Ivan's Blog

Monday 3/02	The first day in my new job! All morning, I filled out forms for the human resources department. In the afternoon, I met the other people on my team and learned how to use the copier and the computer.
Tuesday 3/03	I've been trying very hard to talk to everyone here because it's important to network. I'm not very confident yet, but I have been smiling at everyone and introducing myself. Most people are really friendly. But some are too serious, and they don't say much!
Wednesday 3/04	Today I went to lunch with two of my co-workers. I think I'm starting to make friends here! They told me it's hard work – I'm worried about that, but I'm not going to give up!
Thursday 3/05	Today I was really tired. I almost fell asleep on the train coming home. I was too tired to cook dinner and fell asleep in front of the TV. This job is harder than I expected. I feel a bit depressed.
Friday 3/06	It's been a busy week! I've been learning a lot and I'm excited about learning more. But I'll have to be patient.

If you have any tips about starting a new job – please share them with me!

Check your answers. See page 138.

2 Number the events from Ivan's blog in Exercise 1.

_____ Ivan almost fell asleep on the train home.

_____ Ivan met the other people on his team.

_____ Ivan had lunch with his co-workers.

__1__ Ivan filled out human resources forms.

_____ Ivan was too tired to cook dinner.

_____ Ivan learned how to use the office machines.

3 Match the dates with Ivan's feelings. Use the information in Ivan's blog in Exercise 1.

1. Monday __c__   a. patient and ready to learn

2. Tuesday _____   b. depressed

3. Wednesday _____   c. excited

4. Thursday _____   d. friendly

5. Friday _____   e. a little worried

4 Find the adjectives in Ivan's blog. Underline them. Circle the definition that best fits the reading.

1. confident   (a.) sure about yourself   b. firm

2. serious   a. critical   b. quiet

3. depressed   a. unhappy   b. sick

4. busy   a. filled with people   b. lots of things to do

5. excited   a. nervous   b. happy

6. patient   a. not angry   b. able to wait

5 Complete the chart. Use a dictionary to help you.

Adjective	Noun
1. confident	confidence
2. excited	
3. fair	
4. patient	
5. depressed	

Check your answers. See page 139.

1 Complete the thank-you letter. Use the information in the chart.

Your name	Sarah Bonarelli
Your address	264 West Street, Minneapolis, MN 55404
Today's date	August 15, 2009
Name of interviewer	Ms. Ann Robinson
Interviewer's title	Office Manager
Address of interviewer	City Office Services, 2321 Central Avenue, Minneapolis, MN 55409
Date of interview	August 14, 2009
Reason for saying thank you	Job interview on Friday, August 14th
Something specific you appreciate	You showed me the office and the supply room.

264 West Street _____

_____

_____

_____

_____

_____

_____

_____

Dear _____ :

    I would like to thank you for the _____ I had with you on

_____ . I appreciate the time you spent with me.

Thank you for showing me around the _____ and the

_____ .

    Thank you again for your time. I hope to hear from you soon.

                     Sincerely,

                     _____

Check your answers. See page 139.

2 Tony Wilson went on a job interview. Write Tony's thank-you letter. Use the information from his notes.

Notes
- Interview with Mr. Alan Barlow, Personnel Manager
- December 18, 2009, 10:00 a.m.
- Superstar Electric Company
  465 Main Avenue, Houston, TX 77028
- He told me about the training program.
- He gave me the employee handbook to read. It helped me learn more about the company.

13 New Street
Houston, TX 77297

December 18, 2009

_____

_____

_____

_____

_____

_____ :

_____

_____

_____

_____

_____

_____

_____

_____ ,

_____

Check your answers. See page 139.

Another view

1 Read the questions. Look at the chart. Circle the answers.

Fastest growing occupations 2004–2014

Occupation	Number of new jobs	Percent increase in growth	Required training
home health aides	350,000	56%	short-term on-the-job training
medical assistants	202,000	52%	moderate-term on-the-job training
dental assistants	114,000	43%	moderate-term on-the-job training
paralegals and legal assistants	67,000	30%	associate degree
physical therapist aides	15,000	34%	short-term on-the-job training

Source: U.S. Bureau of Labor Statistics

1. Which job will grow the most from 2004 to 2014?

   a. dental assistants

   b. home health aides

   c. physical therapist aides

   d. paralegals and legal assistants

2. Which job has the second largest number of new jobs?

   a. dental assistants

   b. medical assistants

   c. home health aides

   d. physical therapist aides

3. This chart does NOT give information about _____ .

   a. the type of training required

   b. the percent increase in growth

   c. the number of new jobs in 2004

   d. the number of new jobs from 2004 to 2014

4. What is the increase in the percentage of jobs for dental assistants?

   a. 30%

   b. 34%

   c. 43%

   d. 52%

5. How many new jobs will there be for physical therapist aides from 2004 to 2014?

   a. 15,000

   b. 67,000

   c. 114,000

   d. 202,000

6. Which statement is NOT true?

   a. There will be more new jobs for medical assistants than dental assistants.

   b. There will be more new jobs for home health aides than for dental assistants.

   c. There will be more new jobs for dental assistants than for medical assistants.

   d. There will be more new jobs for dental assistants than for physical therapist aides.

Check your answers. See page 139.

2 Match the job interview questions with answers.

1. What job are you applying for? _b_
2. Tell me about your background. ____
3. Are you currently employed? ____
4. What skills do you have? ____
5. What are your personal strengths? ____
6. Can you work any shift? ____

a. No, I don't have a job right now.
b. I'm applying for a job in computer sales.
c. I'm good at computers and math.
d. I'm helpful and reliable.
e. No, I can't work nights.
f. I'm from Brazil. I've lived in the United States for three years.

3 Read the sentences. Unscramble the words and complete the sentences.

1. Before you apply for a job, do some _____ online.
   (haesrerc)

2. To find out about jobs in your city, you need to _____ with friends and family.
   (twkorne)

3. Practice talking about your skills and your personal _____ .
   (rgtsensht)

4. The job you have now is your _____ job.
   (rtecrun)

5. If you are working, you are _____ .
   (dymepelo)

6. When you apply for a job, you usually need to speak to an _____ .
   (nrevreiweit)

4 Complete the note.

away	down	off	out	up

☕ *Chrissy's Diner*

NOTE TO EMPLOYEES
Before you close up the diner at night:

1. Turn _down_ the heat.
2. Clean _____ the floor.
3. Throw _____ the cups.
4. Fill _____ your time sheet.
5. Turn _____ the lights.

Check your answers. See page 139.

Get ready

1 Complete the conversation.

| broke into | crime | robbed | robber | stole |

Anton Did you hear that someone ___*broke into*___ Arthur's car last
1

night and _____ his computer.
2

Fred That's terrible!

Anton Arthur's really upset. He uses that computer for work, and it

has the names and addresses of his customers in it.

Fred What's he going to do?

Anton Well, the computer has a secret code in it. If the

_____ tries to use it, an alarm will go off and tell
3

the police where it is.

Fred That's smart! By the way, did you hear that someone

_____ the bank on South Street last week?
4

Anton There is so much _____ in this neighborhood now!
5

2 Circle the answers. Use the information in Exercise 1.

1. What happened to Arthur?
   a. Someone stole his car.
   b. Someone stole his computer.
   c. Someone broke into his house.
   d. Someone broke his computer.

2. Why is Arthur upset?
   a. His car is broken.
   b. His car is expensive.
   c. His computer has a special alarm.
   d. His computer has important
      information on it.

3. What will happen if the robber uses
   the computer?
   a. The police will find the car.
   b. The police will find the computer.
   c. The police will call Arthur.
   d. The police will call the robber.

4. What happened at the bank?
   a. Someone left the bank.
   b. Someone closed the bank.
   c. Someone cleaned up the bank.
   d. Someone stole cash from the bank.

Check your answers. See page 139.

3 Complete the paragraph.

crime	mess	robbed	robber	stole

There is too much _____crime_____ in my neighborhood now!
                        1

Someone _____ my purse while I was eating lunch yesterday.
                 2

Someone _____ the bank last night. A _____
                 3   4

took my neighbor's TV, cell phone, and jewelry last week. We went to my

neighbor's house to help him clean up the _____ .
                                                        5

4 Read the police report. Answer the questions.

POLICE REPORT

Case Number: 00988678

Reporting police officer: Randy Thomson

Date of report: September 15, 2010

P O L I C E
D E P A R T M E N T

A robber broke into Mrs. Pilar Rodriguez's home on Monday, September 15, 2010, around 11:30 p.m. The robber got in through a broken window in the bathroom. The robber stole a TV, a DVD player, and a computer.

A worried neighbor called the police at 11:34 p.m. Police arrived at the scene at 11:42 p.m.

I told Mrs. Rodriguez to fix her broken window and always keep her front door locked.

1. What happened at Pilar Rodriguez's home?

   A robber broke into her house.

2. How did the robber get in?

   _____

3. What did the robber steal?

   _____

4. What did Pilar's neighbor do?

   _____

5. What should Pilar do?

   _____

Check your answers. See page 139.

Study the chart and explanation on page 126.

1 Complete the conversations. Use the past continuous.

1. **A** What were you doing last night around 6:00 p.m.?

    B I _____*was eating*_____ dinner.
    (eat)

2. **A** What was Julie doing yesterday afternoon?

    B She _____ her cousin's children.
    (babysit)

3. **A** What were Phuong and Tim doing on Sunday morning?

    B They _____ a neighbor.
    (visit)

4. **A** What were Lisa and Alan doing on Monday night?

    B They _____ the kitchen.
    (clean)

5. **A** What was Kemal doing at 4:30 p.m.?

    B He was _____ a newspaper.
    (read)

2 What were these people doing at 8:00 a.m. yesterday? Complete the sentences.

| drive | knit | sleep | study | talk | watch |

Taline | Aram | Sally | Scott | Leo | Sal

1. Taline _____*was knitting*_____ a sweater. Aram _____*was watching*_____ TV.

2. Sally _____ . Scott _____ on the phone.

3. Leo _____ . Sal _____ to work.

Check your answers. See page 139.

3 Look at the chart. Answer the questions.

	9:00 a.m.	2:00 p.m.	5:00 p.m.
Anna	eat breakfast	study English	clean the house
Pete	paint the bedroom	study English	watch a movie
Louise	drive to work	attend a meeting	clean the house
Fareed	drive to work	read a book	watch a movie

1. **A** Was Louise studying English at 2:00 p.m.?

   B _No, she wasn't._ _____

2. **A** Were Anna and Louise cleaning the house at 5:00 p.m.?

   B _____

3. **A** Were Louise and Fareed driving to work at 9:00 a.m.?

   B _____

4. **A** Was Pete studying English at 5:00 p.m.?

   B _____

4 Write questions and answers. Use the present continuous and the information in the chart in Exercise 3.

1. Anna / 9:00 a.m.

   A What _was Anna doing at 9:00 a.m._ _____ ?

   B _She was eating breakfast._ _____

2. Fareed / 2:00 p.m.

   A What _____ ?

   B _____

3. Pete / 9:00 a.m.

   A What _____ ?

   B _____

4. Anna and Pete / 2:00 p.m.

   A What _____ ?

   B _____

Check your answers. See page 139.

Lesson C *Past continuous and simple past*

Study the explanation on page 129.

1 Underline the past continuous in each sentence.

1. We <u>were jogging</u> in the park when it started to rain.

2. I ran out of gas while I was driving to work.

3. Seema was having lunch with a friend when someone stole her car.

4. When the fire started, I was making cookies in the kitchen.

5. While the neighbors were attending a meeting, someone called the police.

6. Fatima was talking on the phone when her husband came home.

2 Complete the paragraph. Use the past continuous or the simple past.

While I ____*was working*____ in the garden yesterday,
               1. work

I _____*heard*_____ a loud noise in the street. It sounded like a car
        2. hear

accident. When I looked in the street, two strangers _____ .
                                         3. talk

One of them looked very upset. The other driver _____
                                         4. drive

too fast when she _____ a tree. The tree then
                        5. hit

_____ on the other person's car. What a mess!
        6. fall

Check your answers. See page 139.

102 Unit 9

3 Write sentences. Use the past continuous and the simple past.

1. While we (eat lunch), the lights (go out).

   While we were eating lunch, the lights went out.

2. Ellen (sleep) when the fire alarm (go off) in her home.

   _____

3. When we (get) a parking ticket, we (shop) at the mall.

   _____

4. While Francisco (jog), it (start) to rain.

   _____

5. While I (cook) dinner, my husband (attend) a meeting.

   _____

6. Julio and Tia (work) in the garden when Julio (fall) off the ladder.

   _____

4 Combine the sentences. Use the past continuous and the simple past.

1. Chang watched TV. The fire alarm went off.

   While *Chang was watching TV, the fire alarm went off* .

2. The lights went out. We visited our neighbors.

   When _____ , _____ .

3. I baked a cake. An earthquake started.

   _____ when _____ .

4. We ate dinner. A thief stole my purse.

   _____ when _____ .

5. It began to rain. Fernando and Luis painted the house.

   _____ while _____ .

6. We cleaned the house. Our daughter fell out of bed.

   _____ when _____ .

7. Maria took a grammar test. Yan did her homework.

   While _____ , _____ .

8. We ran out of gas. We drove to Boston.

   _____ while _____ .

Check your answers. See page 139.

1 Read the article. Circle the answers.

A Helping Hand

by Rodrigo and Elena Gonzalez

A year ago, a huge hurricane hit our state. It was the largest hurricane in 40 years, and it destroyed many of the homes in our neighborhood. Everyone had to evacuate. Some people lost everything – their home, their furniture, their car. Luckily, our home was OK, but we felt we had to help our neighbors.

The next day, we started to collect money, clothes, shoes, and food. Everyone was very generous and gave as much as they could. We used the money to buy food and water bottles. Two days later, we had three cars full of supplies. We took them over to the park and set up a shelter.

For the next three days, we stayed at the shelter. While people were looking for their families and gathering their things, we cooked food, served tea and coffee, and handed out clothes, food, and water. They were really glad to have our support. And we were very glad to have the chance to help them. One year later, we started a neighborhood organization to help everyone in our community in difficult times. It's important to know you can get help from your neighbors.

1. What is the main idea of this article?
   a. Hurricanes are dangerous.
   b. People should ask for help.
   c. Some people lost everything.
   d. Neighbors should help each other.

2. Which event happened first?
   a. The writers set up a shelter.
   b. The writers bought food and water.
   c. The writers collected food and money.
   d. The writers started a neighborhood organization.

3. What happened when the writers started to collect supplies?
   a. People didn't give any money.
   b. People gave clothes, food, and money.
   c. People gave tents and water bottles.
   d. People did not give very much.

4. Why did the writers feel good?
   a. They had to evacuate.
   b. They got to rebuild their home.
   c. They didn't need help.
   d. They were able to help their neighbors.

Check your answers. See page 140.

2 Underline the time phrases. Answer the questions.

1. We moved to this country <u>in 2006</u>. <u>A year later</u> we had a baby.

   A When did they have a baby?

   B *In 2007.*

2. A hurricane destroyed our home in August. Two months later, we rebuilt our home.

   A When did they rebuild their home?

   B _____

3. In July, there was a terrible fire in our town. For the next three months, we collected money and clothes.

   A When did they stop collecting money and clothes?

   B _____

4. At 6:00 p.m., we heard the fire alarm. Four minutes later, we evacuated the building.

   A At what time did they evacuate the building?

   B _____

3 Match the **bold** words with the correct meaning.

1. a. They were **gathering** apples in the backyard.
   b. A crowd of people was **gathering** in the street.

   _b_ meeting   _a_ collecting

2. a. Daniel needs a job to **support** his family.
   b. Thank you for your **support** after the hurricane.

   _____ help   _____ pay for

3. a. A thief **grabbed** my wallet on the bus.
   b. I **grabbed** as many photographs as I could during the fire.

   _____ stole   _____ took quickly

4. a. They gave us a **generous** amount of money.
   b. Our neighbors were very **generous** to us after the earthquake.

   _____ large   _____ helpful

5. a. We **lost** everything in the earthquake.
   b. We **lost** the game.

   _____ didn't win   _____ don't have it anymore

Check your answers. See page 140.

1 Read the story. Answer the questions.

One evening last week, I was driving home from work. I was driving slowly through my neighborhood when my cell phone rang. It was my wife. She asked me to pick up some food from the supermarket for dinner on the way home. I was turning off my cell phone when a cat ran across the street. I immediately turned the car to the right, and I hit a fire hydrant. Water went everywhere.

Luckily, I was OK. I didn't hit the cat, but the car was damaged. Firefighters came to fix the fire hydrant. The police arrived, and I had to fill out an accident report. While I was talking to the police, my wife called again. She wanted to know what happened to me. I said, "Well, I think I'll be a little late tonight."

1. What is the story about?

   The story is about a car accident.

2. When did the accident happen?

   _____

3. Where did the accident happen?

   _____

4. What was the writer doing when the story started?

   _____

5. Why did the accident happen?

   _____

6. How did the story end?

   _____

Check your answers. See page 140.

2 Look at the pictures. Circle the answers.

1. When did the story start?   a. at 5:55 a.m.   **b. at 5:55 p.m.**

2. Where did the story happen?   a. on a train   b. on a plane

3. What was Joe doing when the
   story started?   a. reading   b. talking

4. What was next to Joe?   a. a friend   b. a box

5. What happened while he was
   getting off the train?   a. He found his box.   b. He saw a friend.

6. What happened when the
   train doors closed?   a. He remembered his box.   b. He forgot his book.

7. How did the story end?   a. The doors opened,   b. The doors closed,
                                                    and he took his box.   and he lost his box.

3 Write a paragraph about what happened to the man in the pictures from Exercise 2. Use the past continuous. Write one sentence with *when* and one sentence with *while*.

One evening at 5:55 p.m., Joe was sitting on a train.

_____

_____

_____

_____

_____

_____

_____

Check your answers. See page 140.

Another view

1 Read the questions. Look at the chart. Circle the answers.

Top ten cities in the U.S. in rank order by population size		
	1990	2000
New York, NY	1	1
Los Angeles, CA	2	2
Chicago, IL	3	3
Houston, TX	4	4
Philadelphia, PA	5	5
Phoenix, AZ	9	6
San Diego, CA	6	7
Dallas, TX	8	8
San Antonio, TX	10	9
Detroit, MI	7	10

Sources: U.S. Census Bureau. http://www.census.gov/statab/ccdb/cit1020r.txt and
http://www.census.gov/population/www/documentation/twps0027.html

1. Which state has the highest number of top ten cities by population size?
   a. Texas
   b. Arizona
   c. California
   d. New York

2. Which city had the same ranking in 1990 and in 2000?
   a. Detroit
   b. Phoenix
   c. San Antonio
   d. Los Angeles

3. Which city had a different ranking?
   a. New York
   b. Houston
   c. San Diego
   d. Philadelphia

4. Which city's rank order changed the most?
   a. Chicago
   b. Dallas
   c. Phoenix
   d. San Diego

5. What information is *not* in the chart?
   a. the U.S. cities with the greatest population in 2000
   b. the number of people in the top ten U.S. cities in 2000
   c. the U.S. cities with the greatest population in 1990
   d. the rank order by population size of the top ten U.S. cities in 1990

Check your answers. See page 140.

2 Match.

1. fire _e_
2. smoke ____
3. emergency ____
4. first-aid ____
5. neighborhood ____

a. alarm
b. watch
c. kit
d. exit
e. extinguisher

3 Complete the sentences. Use the words from Exercise 2.

1. You will need a _____ _first-aid kit_ _____ if you are hurt.
2. This building map will help you find the nearest _____ .
3. A _____ tells you there is smoke nearby.
4. You can use a _____ if there is a small fire in your kitchen.
5. If we have a _____ , we'll feel safer in our community.

4 Match the parts of the pictures. What are they?

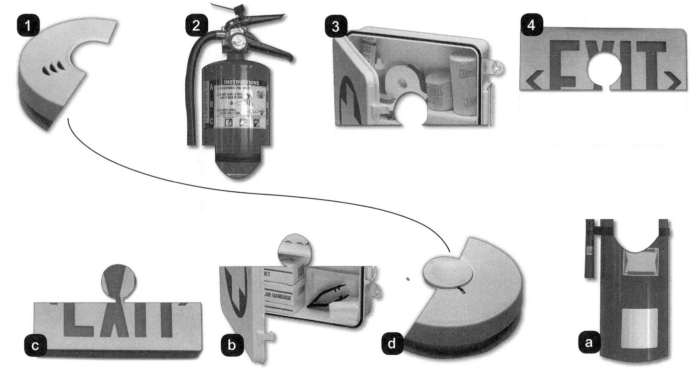

1 + _d_ = _____ _smoke alarm_ _____

2 + ____ = _____

3 + ____ = _____

4 + ____ = _____

Check your answers. See page 140.

Get ready

1 Make sentences. Match the sentence parts.

1. You should reserve a room early ___c___
2. You should book a flight in advance _____
3. The advertised room rate _____
4. Before you go camping, _____
5. Many tourists _____

a. you should reserve a campsite.
b. come here during the summer.
c. because hotels are very busy at this time.
d. to get the best discounts.
e. doesn't usually include tax.

2 Complete the paragraph.

books	days off	discounts	reserve	round-trip	tax

Fabiola has three _____*days off*_____ next week. She wants
to go on vacation. She went on the Internet and found some good

_____ on flights to Washington, D.C. She can get a

_____ ticket for $85.00 if she _____ her

flight five days ahead. The flight takes one hour. It leaves at 2:00 p.m. on

Monday, and the return flight leaves Washington, D.C., at 11:00 a.m. on

Wednesday. The hotel costs $120 a night plus _____ , which is

$14.50 per night.

If she takes the train, the trip will take three hours. The train leaves at

8:00 a.m. on Monday, and the return train leaves Washington, D.C., at

6:00 p.m. on Tuesday. She does not need to _____ a hotel

room for two nights. The train costs $234.00, but she can stay just one night

and still have two full days of sightseeing.

3 Complete the chart. Use the information in Exercise 2.

	Cost of transportation	Cost of lodging	Total cost
By plane	$85.00		
By train			

It is cheaper for Fabiola to travel by _____ .

Check your answers. See page 140.

4 Look at the **bold** words. Write the sentences. Use words from the box with a similar meaning.

days off	discount	high	most popular	reserve

1. Room rates are **expensive** in the summer. *Room rates are high in the summer.*

2. Summer is the **busiest** season for tourists. _____

3. You can get a **cheaper rate** if you book ahead. _____

4. You can **book** your hotel room online. _____

5. Sam has three **vacation days**. _____

5 Solve the problems.

1. Sal and Dana need a vacation. They want to take a weekend trip to Miami. They have never been there before. They can get a round-trip plane ticket for $150.00 each. They will share the hotel room. It costs $150.00 per night plus tax. The tax is $19.00 dollars per night. How much will their transportation and lodging cost?

   Round-trip tickets for two $ *300.00*

   Lodging for two nights $ _____

   Room tax for two nights $ _____

   Total $ _____

2. Joanna and Andy have a few days off and they want to take a vacation. They have $950.00 to spend on transportation and lodging. They want to go to Orlando for three nights. Round-trip plane tickets cost $250.00 for each person. They will share the hotel room. It costs $120.00 per night plus $13.00 for tax each night. How much money will they have after they have paid for transportation and lodging?

   Round-trip tickets for two $ _____

   Hotel for three nights $ _____

   Room tax for three nights $ _____

   Total $ _____

   Money they will have $ _____

Check your answers. See page 140.

Study the explanation on page 129.

1 Circle the correct forms of the verbs.

1. If we **get** / **will get** a few days off, we **go** / **will go** to the beach.
2. Rosa **travels** / **will travel** by plane if the tickets **aren't** / **won't be** too expensive.
3. If the weather **is** / **will be** good, we **ride** / **will ride** our bicycles.
4. If Charlie **visits** / **will visit** San Diego, he **stays** / **will stay** with his sister.
5. If we **don't** / **won't** find a cheap hotel, we **don't** / **won't** go to New York.

2 Look at the pictures. Answer the questions.

1. What will Jack do if his friends come over this afternoon?

   If Jack's friends come over this afternoon, they'll play soccer.

2. What will the Perez family do if the weather is good?

   _____

3. What will Stacey do if she has the day off?

   _____

4. What will Robert do this weekend if it rains?

   _____

Check your answers. See page 140.

3 Complete the conversation. Use the simple present or future form of the verbs.

A What will you do this summer if you have a few days off?

B If I _____*have*_____ enough money, I _____
             1. have   2. visit
my family in California.

A That sounds fun! What _____ you _____ if you _____
                                   3. do   4. not / have
enough money?

B I guess I'll stay home. What about you?

A If my brother _____ from Chicago, we _____
                         5. come   6. go
camping. But if he _____ , I _____
                     7. not / come   8. visit
my friends in Houston.

4 Write questions with *if*. Then answer the questions.

1. Brian / do / have time off this summer

   A What *will Brian do if he has time off this summer* _____ ?

   B He *will go swimming* _____ .
                      (go swimming)

2. Tam and Chen / do / the weather is beautiful this weekend

   A What _____ ?

   B They _____ .
                    (work in the garden)

3. Sara / do / get some extra money for her birthday

   A What _____ ?

   B She _____ .
                    (go shopping)

4. you / do / have a three-day weekend

   A What _____ ?

   B I _____ .
                    (go hiking)

5. we / do / the weather is bad

   A What _____ ?

   B We _____ .
                    (clean the house)

6. Anna / do / find a cheap flight

   A What _____ ?

   B She _____ .
                    (fly to Seattle)

Check your answers. See page 141.

Dependent clauses

Study the explanation on page 129.

1 Complete the sentences. Use the correct form of the verb.

Sanjit is planning a trip to Colorado. He has decided to make a list of things he needs to do before he ___*leaves*___ .
1. leave

Before he _____ on his trip, he
2. go

_____ some books about Colorado.
3. read

After he _____ the books, he
4. read

_____ a map and choose the best
5. find

route for his trip. He _____ some campsites and make reservations
6. choose

before he _____ . On the day before he _____ , he _____
7. leave   8. leave   9. buy

some food and first-aid supplies. He _____ some gas at the gas station,
10. get

too. After he does all that, he _____ his baggage into the car. Then he'll
11. put

be ready for his trip!

2 Complete the sentences. Use the simple present or future with *will*.

1. Victor / book a flight to Dallas / talk to a travel agent

   Before *Victor books a flight to Dallas* , *he will talk to a travel agent* .

2. Victor / make a hotel reservation / fly to Dallas

   _____ before _____ .

3. Victor / clean up the house / leave for the airport

   After _____ , _____ .

4. Victor / go through security / check in

   _____ after _____ .

5. Victor / return from his trip / buy presents for his family

   Before _____ , _____ .

Check your answers. See page 141.

3 Look at Pedro's calendar. Write sentences about his plans. Use *before* and *after*.

Monday, November 26		Tuesday, November 27	
9:30–5:30 p.m.	Work	9:30–5:30 p.m.	Work
6:00 p.m.	Buy concert tickets	6:15 p.m.	Meet Nick
7:00 p.m.	Invite Nick to the concert	6:30 p.m.	Eat dinner at a restaurant
7:30 p.m.	Make dinner reservations	8:30 p.m.	Concert

1. Pedro / buy the concert tickets / invite Nick to the concert

   a. *Pedro will buy concert tickets before he invites Nick to the concert.*

   b. *Pedro will invite Nick to the concert after he buys concert tickets.*

2. He / invite Nick to the concert / make dinner reservations

   a. *He will invite Nick to the concert before* _____

   b. *He will make dinner reservations after* _____

3. He / meet Nick / finish work

   a. _____

   b. _____

4. He / go to the concert / eat dinner at a restaurant

   a. _____

   b. _____

4 Complete the conversations. Use the word in parentheses.

1. **A** What *will you do before you go on your trip* _____ ? (before)

   B Before I go on my trip, I will learn a few words in French.

2. **A** What *will Trina do before* _____ ? (before)

   B Before Trina goes on vacation, she will get a passport.

3. **A** Where _____ ? (after)

   B They will go to Philadelphia after they leave New York.

4. **A** What _____ ? (before)

   B Suzanna will buy a cup of coffee before she reads the newspaper.

5. **A** Where _____ ? (after)

   B Danh and Giang will go to a concert after they cook dinner.

Check your answers. See page 141.

3 Look at Pedro's calendar. Write sentences about his plans. Use *before* and *after*.

Monday, November 26		Tuesday, November 27	
9:30–5:30 p.m.	Work	9:30–5:30 p.m.	Work
6:00 p.m.	Buy concert tickets	6:15 p.m.	Meet Nick
7:00 p.m.	Invite Nick to the concert	6:30 p.m.	Eat dinner at a restaurant
7:30 p.m.	Make dinner reservations	8:30 p.m.	Concert

1. Pedro / buy the concert tickets / invite Nick to the concert
   a. _Pedro will buy concert tickets before he invites Nick to the concert._
   b. _Pedro will invite Nick to the concert after he buys concert tickets._

2. He / invite Nick to the concert / make dinner reservations
   a. _He will invite Nick to the concert before_
   b. _He will make dinner reservations after_

3. He / meet Nick / finish work
   a. _____
   b. _____

4. He / go to the concert / eat dinner at a restaurant
   a. _____
   b. _____

4 Complete the conversations. Use the word in parentheses.

1. **A** What _will you do before you go on your trip_ ? (before)
   B Before I go on my trip, I will learn a few words in French.

2. **A** What _will Trina do before_ ? (before)
   B Before Trina goes on vacation, she will get a passport.

3. **A** Where _____ ? (after)
   B They will go to Philadelphia after they leave New York.

4. **A** What _____ ? (before)
   B Suzanna will buy a cup of coffee before she reads the newspaper.

5. **A** Where _____ ? (after)
   B Danh and Giang will go to a concert after they cook dinner.

Check your answers. See page 141.

1 Read the article. Circle *T* (true) or *F* (false).

The Statue of Liberty

The Statue of Liberty is one of the most popular tourist sights in New York City and a symbol of freedom for many Americans. The statue is on Liberty Island in the middle of New York Harbor. The people of France gave the statue to the people of the United States in 1886 as a gift of friendship.

Many people call the statue by its popular name, "Lady Liberty." The statue is a woman wearing a long robe and a crown with seven points. The points represent the seven continents and seven seas. She holds a flat piece of stone in her left hand and a burning torch high in her right hand. The stone has the date "JULY IV MDCCLXXVI" (July 4, 1776), the day of America's independence from Britain.

There are 354 steps inside the statue and 25 windows in the crown. The 25 windows represent the 25 natural minerals of the earth. The inside used to be open to the public. Visitors arrived by ferry and climbed the stairs inside the statue. About 30 people could climb all the way up into her crown at one time. They had a wonderful view of New York Harbor. Admission was free, but the waiting time outside was usually more than three hours.

Today, the crown of the statue is closed, but the island is open. You can visit the museum and the base of the statue if you have a Time Pass. There are a limited number of tickets sold every day, and tickets often sell out. You can buy them in advance and pick them up before you board the ferry.

1. The article gives information about the history of the statue.	(T)	F
2. The article describes the statue.	T	F
3. The article gives information about how to visit the statue.	T	F
4. The statue is over 300 years old.	T	F
5. The torch is in Lady Liberty's left hand.	T	F
6. France gave the statue as a gift in 1776.	T	F
7. Lady Liberty's crown has seven points.	T	F
8. You cannot buy tickets in advance to see the Statue of Liberty.	T	F

Check your answers. See page 141.

2 Answer the questions. Use the information in Exercise 1.

1. What is the main topic of the article?

   The Statue of Liberty is the main topic of this article.

2. Where is the statue located?

   _____

3. What happened in 1886?

   _____

4. Why did the people of France give the statue to the United States?

   _____

5. Why does July 4, 1776, appear on the statue?

   _____

6. How many steps are inside the statue?

   _____

7. What could you see from inside the crown?

   _____

8. What do you need if you want to visit the museum?

   _____

3 Scan the article for the **bold** words. Circle the words with a similar meaning.

1. **sights**
   a. attractions
   b. parks

2. **symbol**
   a. sign
   b. gift

3. **gift**
   a. promise
   b. present

4. **robe**
   a. dress
   b. jacket

5. **torch**
   a. pen
   b. fire

6. **independence**
   a. freedom
   b. friendship

7. **pass**
   a. entrance
   b. ticket

8. **board**
   a. get on
   b. get off

Check your answers. See page 141.

1 Read the paragraph. Answer the questions.

Central Park

Central Park, one of the most popular tourist attractions in New York City, is popular because it offers something for everyone. It is right in the heart of the city and is a perfect place to relax after a shopping trip or before you go to the theater. The zoo is open every day. If your children like animals, they will love the children's zoo, where children can touch animals such as goats and sheep. Older children can go to a beginner climbing course with special indoor and outdoor climbing walls. If the weather is nice, you can enjoy the beautiful weather and row boats on the lake. If you love culture and music, you'll enjoy one of the concerts or a theater performance of Shakespeare in the open-air theater. Finally, if you feel tired after a day of sightseeing and shopping, you can take a relaxing and romantic ride around the park in a horse-drawn carriage.

1. What is the main idea of the paragraph?

   Central Park is a popular attraction because it offers something for everyone.

2. What are four examples of things to do in Central Park?

   a. _____

   b. _____

   c. _____

   d. _____

3. What is the conclusion?

   _____

Check your answers. See page 141.

2 Read the information. Then write a paragraph about Hollywood. Include a main idea, at least three examples of things to do in Hollywood, and a conclusion.

One of the most popular tourist attractions in California is Hollywood. Hollywood has something for everyone.

Check your answers. See page 141.

Another view

1 Read the questions. Look at the amusement park information. Circle the answers.

	Family Fun Amusement Park	Great Days Away Amusement Park
Admission	One-day adult admission $34.95 Junior (3–8) $24.95 Senior (55+) $27.95 Children under 3 are free	One-day adult admission $24.95 Junior (5–12) $14.95 Senior (65+) $19.95 Children under 5 are free
Amenities	Water rides and family rides Indoor and outdoor swimming pools 4 movie theaters Restaurants / cafés	Mini-golf and go-kart racing Climbing courses for all ages Child play center Restaurants / cafés
Restaurants	Price Range • Appetizers: $5.00–$7.50 • Main courses: $8.99–$15.00 • Desserts: $4.75–$7.50	Price Range • Appetizers: $5.00–$15.00 • Main courses: $12.00–$24.00 • Desserts: $5.50–$8.00
Driving distance from destinations	San Francisco, CA (2 hours) Los Angeles, CA (6 hours)	Boston, MA (4 hours) Washington, DC (5 hours)

1. What is the admission for a person aged 66 at Family Fun Amusement Park?
   a. $19.95
   b. $24.95
   c. $27.95
   d. $34.95

2. Which is the cheapest?
   a. one junior admission at Family Fun
   b. one junior admission at Great Days Away
   c. one senior admission at Family Fun
   d. one senior admission at Great Days Away

3. Which statement is true?
   a. Children under five are free at Family Fun.
   b. Children over three are free at Family Fun.
   c. Children over three are free at Great Days Away.
   d. Children under five are free at Great Days Away.

4. How far is Great Days Away from Boston?
   a. 1.5 hours
   b. 4 hours
   c. 4.5 hours
   d. 6 hours

5. Which statement is true?
   a. Great Days Away has a child play center.
   b. Great Days Away has a movie theater.
   c. Family Fun has a climbing course.
   d. Family Fun has mini-golf.

6. How much is the most expensive main course at Family Fun?
   a. $8.99
   b. $12.00
   c. $15.00
   d. $24.00

Check your answers. See page 141.

2 Read the information. Answer the questions. Some answers may appear more than once.

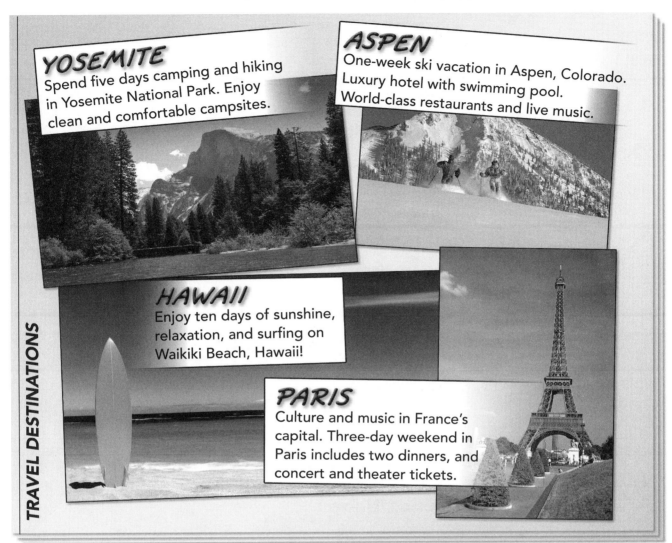

TRAVEL DESTINATIONS

YOSEMITE
Spend five days camping and hiking in Yosemite National Park. Enjoy clean and comfortable campsites.

ASPEN
One-week ski vacation in Aspen, Colorado. Luxury hotel with swimming pool. World-class restaurants and live music.

HAWAII
Enjoy ten days of sunshine, relaxation, and surfing on Waikiki Beach, Hawaii!

PARIS
Culture and music in France's capital. Three-day weekend in Paris includes two dinners, and concert and theater tickets.

Pepi hates swimming and skiing. He's not interested in art or music. He loves camping and hiking. He has one week's vacation.

Eve loves going to museums and art galleries. She also likes going to musical events and eating out in restaurants. She doesn't like skiing and outdoor activities.

Sebastien loves skiing, snowboarding, and all kinds of winter sports. He hates hiking, though, and can only take off three days. He enjoys music and art.

Paulina loves swimming, surfing, and warm weather. She doesn't like camping or visiting museums.

1. Where should Pepi go on vacation? _Yosemite National Park_

2. Where should Eve go on vacation? _____

3. Where should Sebastien go on vacation? _____

4. Where should Paulina go on vacation? _____

5. Which two people should take a trip together? _____

Check your answers. See page 141.

Verbs + gerunds

A gerund is the base form of a verb + -ing.
Gerunds often follow verbs that talk about preferences. Use a gerund like a noun.

Spelling rules for gerunds
• Verbs ending in a vowel-consonant pair repeat the consonant before adding -ing:

stop → stopping   get → getting

• Verbs ending in silent -e drop the e before -ing:

dance → dancing   exercise → exercising

but:

be → being   see → seeing

Questions

Do	I you we they	enjoy dancing?
Does	he she it	

Affirmative statements

I You We They	enjoy	dancing.
He She It	enjoys	

Negative statements

I You We They	don't enjoy	dancing.
He She It	doesn't enjoy	

Verbs often followed by gerunds (verb + -ing)

avoid	feel like	love	quit
can't help	finish	mind	recommend
dislike	hate	miss	regret
enjoy	like	practice	suggest

Gerunds after prepositions

Prepositions are words like in, of, about, and for. Prepositions are often used in phrases with adjectives (excited about, interested in) and verbs (think about). Gerunds often follow these phrases.

Wh- questions: What

What	am	I	tired of doing?
	are	you we they	
	is	he she it	

Affirmative statements

I	am	tired of working.
You We They	are	
He She It	is	

Phrases with prepositions

afraid of	famous for	nervous about	thank (someone) for
amazed by	good at	plan on	think about
angry at	happy about	pleased about	tired of
bad at	interested in	sad about	worried about
excited about	look forward to	talk about	

Verbs + infinitives

An infinitive is *to* + the base form of a verb.
Infinitives often follow certain verbs. See below for a list of verbs
that infinitives often follow.

Wh- questions: *Where*

Where	do	I you we they	want to go?
	does	he she it	

Affirmative statements

	I You We They	want to go	to the park.
	He She It	wants to go	

Yes / No questions

Do	I you we they	want to go?
Does	he she it	

Short answers

Yes,	I you we they	do.
	he she it	does.

No,	I you we they	don't.
	he she it	doesn't.

don't = do not
doesn't = does not

Verbs often followed by infinitives

agree	hope	need	promise
can / can't afford	intend	offer	refuse
decide	learn	plan	volunteer
expect	manage	prepare	want
help	mean	pretend	would like

Present perfect

The present perfect is *have* or *has* + past participle.

Use the present perfect to talk about actions that started in the past and continue to now.

See page 151 for a list of past participles with irregular verbs.

Use *how long* + present perfect to ask about the length of time.

Use *for* with a period of time to answer questions with *how long*.

Use *since* with a point in time to answer questions with *how long*.

Wh- questions: *How long*

How long	have	I you we they	been	here?
	has	he she it	been	

Affirmative statements: *for* and *since*

I You We They	have been	here	for two hours. since 6:00 p.m.
He She It	has been		

Use *ever* with the present perfect to ask *Yes / No* questions about things that happened at any time before now.

Yes / No questions: *ever*

Have	I you we they	ever	been late?
Has	he she it	ever	been late?

Short answers

Yes,	I you we they	have.	No,	I you we they	haven't.
Yes,	he she it	has.	No,	he she it	hasn't.

haven't = have not
hasn't = has not

Use *recently* and *lately* with the present perfect to talk about things that happened in the very recent past, not very long ago.

Yes / No questions: *recently* and *lately*

Have	I you we they	gone	to the movies recently? to the movies lately?
Has	he she it		

Present perfect continuous

The present perfect continuous is *have* or *has* + *been* + present participle.
Use the present perfect continuous to talk about actions that started in the past,
continue to now, and will probably continue in the future.

Yes / No questions

Have	I you we they	been working for a long time?
Has	he she it	

Short answers

Yes,	I you we they	have.
	he she it	has.

No,	I you we they	haven't.
	he she it	hasn't.

Wh- questions: *How long*

How long	have	I you we they	been working?
	has	he she it	

Affirmative statements: *for* and *since*

I You We They	have been working	for a month. since October.
He She It	has been working	

used to

Used to talks about things that happened in the past.
Use *used to* to talk about a past situation or past habit that is not true now.

Yes / No questions

Did	I you he she it we you they	use to eat a lot?

Short answers

Yes,	I you he she it we you they	did.

No,	I you he she it we you they	didn't.

didn't = did not

Affirmative statements

I You He She It We You They	used to eat a lot.

Past continuous

Use the past continuous to talk about actions that were happening at a specific time in the past. The actions were not completed at that time.

Wh- questions: What

What	was	I	doing?
	were	you we they	
	was	he she it	

Affirmative statements

I	was	working.
You We They	were	
He She It	was	

Yes / No questions

Was	I	
Were	you we they	working?
Was	he she it	

Short answers

Yes,	I	was.
	you we they	were.
	he she it	was.

No,	I	wasn't.
	you we they	weren't.
	he she it	wasn't.

wasn't = was not
weren't = were not

could and should

Wh- questions: What

What	could should	I you he she it we you they	do?

Affirmative statements

I You He She It We You They	could should	work.

Negative statements

I You He She It We You They	couldn't shouldn't	work.

couldn't = could not
shouldn't = should not

Irregular verbs

Base form	Simple past	Past participle	Base form	Simple past	Past participle
be	was / were	been	leave	left	left
become	became	become	lose	lost	lost
begin	began	begun	make	made	made
break	broke	broken	meet	met	met
bring	brought	brought	pay	paid	paid
build	built	built	put	put	put
buy	bought	bought	read	read	read
catch	caught	caught	ride	rode	ridden
choose	chose	chosen	run	ran	run
come	came	come	say	said	said
cost	cost	cost	see	saw	seen
cut	cut	cut	sell	sold	sold
do	did	done	send	sent	sent
drink	drank	drunk	set	set	set
drive	drove	driven	show	showed	shown
eat	ate	eaten	sing	sang	sung
fall	fell	fallen	sit	sat	sat
feel	felt	felt	sleep	slept	slept
fight	fought	fought	speak	spoke	spoken
find	found	found	spend	spent	spent
fly	flew	flown	stand	stood	stood
forget	forgot	forgotten	steal	stole	stolen
get	got	gotten / got	swim	swam	swum
give	gave	given	take	took	taken
go	went	gone	teach	taught	taught
have	had	had	tell	told	told
hear	heard	heard	think	thought	thought
hide	hid	hidden	throw	threw	thrown
hit	hit	hit	understand	understood	understood
hold	held	held	wake	woke	woken
hurt	hurt	hurt	wear	wore	worn
keep	kept	kept	win	won	won
know	knew	known	write	wrote	written

Spelling rules for regular past participles

- To form the past participle of regular verbs, add -ed to the base form:
  listen → listened
- For regular verbs ending in a consonant + -y, change y to i and add -ed:
  study → studied
- For regular verbs ending in a vowel + -y, add -ed:
  play → played
- For regular verbs ending in -e, add -d:
  live → lived

Grammar explanations

Separable phrasal verbs

A phrasal verb is a verb + preposition. The meaning of the phrasal verb is different from the meaning of the verb alone.

He *handed out* the papers to the class. = He *gave* the papers to the class.

A separable phrasal verb can have a noun between the verb and the preposition.

He *handed **the papers** out*.

A separable phrasal verb can have a pronoun between the verb and the preposition.

He *handed **them** out*.

Separable phrasal verbs

call back	cut off	find out	look up	throw away / out
call up	do over	give back	pick out	turn down
clean up	fill in	hand in	put away / back	turn off
cross out	fill out	hand out	shut off	turn up
cut down	fill up	leave on	tear up	

Comparisons

Use *more than*, *less than*, and *as much as* to compare nouns. A gerund is often used as a noun. You can compare activities by using gerunds and *more than*, *less than*, and *as much as*.

I enjoy *walking more than driving*.
She likes *cooking less than eating*.
They enjoy *singing as much as dancing*.

Giving reasons and explanations with *because* and *because of*

Use a *because* clause to give explanations.

A *because* clause is the part of the sentence that begins with *because* + subject + verb or *because of* + noun phrase. Use a comma (,) when the *because* clause begins the sentence.

I came to Ohio *because of my children*.
Because of my children, I came to Ohio.

I came to Ohio *because my children are here*.
Because my children are here, I came to Ohio.

Adjectives with *enough* and *too*

Use an adjective + *enough* to talk about the right amount of something.

The ladder is *tall enough* to reach the ceiling.

Use *not* + adjective + *enough* to talk about less than the right amount.

The ladder is *not tall enough*.

Use *too* + adjective to talk about more than the right amount.

The ladder is *too tall*.

Dependent clauses

A clause is a part of a sentence that has a subject and a verb. A dependent clause often begins with time words such as *when*, *before*, and *after*. The dependent clause can come at the beginning or end of a sentence. Use a comma (,) after dependent clauses that come at the beginning of a sentence. Do not use a comma when a dependent clause comes at the end of a sentence.

when: Use *when* + present time verbs to talk about habits.

> *When I have a lot to do,* I make a to-do list.
> I make a to-do list *when I have a lot to do.*

after: Use *after* to order events in a sentence. *After* introduces the first event. Use *after* with the simple present to talk about habits.

> First, I eat dinner. Second, I watch the news. =
> I watch the news *after I eat dinner.*
> *After I eat dinner,* I watch the news.

Use *after* with the simple present and future to talk about future plans.

> First, he'll finish school. Second, he'll take a vacation. =
> He'll take a vacation *after he finishes school.*
> *After he finishes school,* he'll take a vacation.

before: Use *before* to order events in a sentence. *Before* introduces the second event. Use *before* with the simple present to talk about habits.

> First, she reads the newspaper. Second, she eats breakfast. =
> She reads the newspaper *before she eats breakfast.*
> *Before she eats breakfast,* she reads the newspaper.

Use *before* with the simple present and future to talk about future plans.

> First, he'll finish school. Second, he'll take a vacation. =
> He'll finish school *before he takes a vacation.*
> *Before he takes a vacation,* he'll finish school.

when and **while**: Use *when* or *while* with the past continuous and simple past to show that one past action interrupted another past action.
Use *when* with the simple past for the action that interrupted.

> They were sleeping *when the fire started.*
> *When the fire started,* they were sleeping.

Use *while* with the past continuous to show the action that was happening before the interruption.

> The fire started *while they were sleeping.*
> *While they were sleeping,* the fire started.

if: Use *if* clauses to talk about future possibility. Use the simple present in the clause with *if*. Use the future in the other clause to talk about what could happen.

> She won't go *if the weather is bad.*
> *If the weather is bad,* she won't go.

Answer key

Unit 1: Personal information

Lesson A: Get ready

Exercise 1 page 2

1. a 2. c 3. b 4. c 5. a 6. c

Exercise 2 page 3

1. party animal
2. outgoing
3. enjoys
4. going out
5. dislikes
6. dance club
7. shy
8. alone

Exercise 3 page 3

1. dislikes
2. enjoys
3. enjoys
4. dislikes
5. dislikes
6. enjoys

Exercise 4 page 3

1. outgoing
2. quiet
3. stay home
4. different
5. dislikes

Lesson B: Verbs + gerunds

Exercise 1 page 4

1. getting up early
2. doing homework
3. doing homework
4. playing soccer
5. playing soccer
6. getting up early

Exercise 2 page 4

1. Yes, he does.
2. No, she doesn't.
3. No, he doesn't.
4. Yes, they do.
5. No, he doesn't.
6. No, he doesn't.

Exercise 3 page 5

1. going out
2. being
3. working
4. reading
5. listening
6. doing
7. playing
8. surfing

Exercise 4 page 5

1A. going out
1B. Yes, he does.
2A. being
2B. Yes, he does.
3A. reading
3B. No, he doesn't.
4A. doing
4B. No, he doesn't.

Exercise 5 page 5

1. Do you enjoy going to the beach?
2. Do you dislike standing in line?
3. Do you like playing cards?
4. Do you mind taking out the garbage?

Lesson C: Comparisons

Exercise 1 page 6

1. playing sports or socializing with friends
2. socializing with friends or playing sports
3. dancing
4. cooking
5. watching movies
6. reading

Exercise 2 page 6

1. Angelina likes watching movies less than cooking.
2. Angelina likes watching movies more than reading.
3. Angelina likes cooking less than dancing.
4. Angelina likes socializing more than dancing.
5. Angelina likes playing sports as much as socializing.

Exercise 3 page 7

1. Ling likes painting more than playing an instrument.
2. Frank enjoys riding a bike more than driving a car.
3. Suzanne enjoys reading more than washing the dishes.
4. Annie and Steve like going to the movies more than shopping.

Exercise 4 page 7

1. Annie and Steve like shopping less *than* watching movies.
2. Ling likes playing an instrument *less* than painting.
3. Suzanna enjoys washing dishes less *than* reading.
4. Frank enjoys driving a car *less* than riding a bike.

Lesson D: Reading

Exercise 1 page 8

1. architect
2. computer programmer
3. teacher

Exercise 2 page 8

1. architect
2. computer programmer
3. teacher
4. computer programmer
5. teacher
6. architect

Exercise 3 page 9

Computer programmers: find answers to problems, like working alone
Teachers: help students, like learning about other people
Architects: design new things, imagine new ideas

Exercise 4 page 9

1. personality
2. intellectual
3. creative
4. artist
5. friendly
6. type
7. outgoing

Lesson E: Writing

Exercise 1 page 10

Jobs: architect, designer, scientist, social worker, teacher
Personality adjectives: creative, friendly, helpful, outgoing, quiet
Activities: drawing, finding answers, helping people, surfing the Internet, talking

Exercise 2 page 10

Name: Peter Jones
Job: social worker
Place of work: community center
Personality: friendly and outgoing
Likes: meeting and helping people

Exercise 3 page 11

1. computer programmer
2. intellectual
3. hardworking
4. finding answers

Exercise 4 page 11

Answer may vary. Possible answer:

Romano Pereira's job fits his personality. He's an architect. He works at New Designs Company in Raleigh, North Carolina. Romano is creative and helpful. He enjoys drawing, and he likes imagining things that are new and different. An architect is a good job for him because it fits his personality.

Lesson F: Another view

Exercise 1 page 12

1. c 2. a 3. a 4. d 5. c 6. b

Exercise 2 page 13

Creative personality: drawing, painting pictures, taking photos
Intellectual personality: doing crossword puzzles, playing chess, reading books
Outgoing personality: going to dance clubs, going to parties, socializing

Exercise 3 page 13

Across	Down
1. artist	2. intellectual
3. outgoing	5. quiet
4. creative	6. shy
7. architect	

Unit 2: At school

Lesson A: Get ready

Exercise 1 page 14

1. paper   4. index cards
2. list   5. concentrate
3. underline   6. discouraged

Exercise 2 page 14

1. b 2. c 3. b 4. a

Exercise 3 page 15

1. d 2. a 3. f 4. e 5. b 6. c

Exercise 4 page 15

1. to-do list   5. underline
2. paper   6. index cards
3. concentrate 7. boring
4. active   8. discouraged

Exercise 5 page 15

Bad study habits: doesn't concentrate, doesn't study new words, is late for class, hands in homework late, forgets homework, doesn't study for the test
Good study habits: Makes a to-do list, hands in homework on time, writes new words on index cards, underlines the main ideas

Lesson B: Present perfect

Exercise 1 page 16

1. for   4. for   7. for
2. since   5. since   8. since
3. since   6. since

Exercise 2 page 16

1. have   3. have   5. has
2. have   4. has   6. have

Exercise 3 page 16

1. has worked   4. has had
2. have lived   5. has taught
3. have studied 6. has been

Exercise 4 page 17

1A. has he been
1B. four hours, 3:00 p.m.
2A. has she known
2B. four months, August 1
3A. has he lived
3B. two years, June 25, 2007

Exercise 5 page 17

1. have they worked in this school
2. has she had a driver's license
3. has he lived in this apartment
4. have you been married

Lesson C: Present perfect

Exercise 1 page 18

1. lost   4. taken
2. forgotten 5. gotten
3. read

Exercise 2 page 18

1A. has, studied
1B. Yes, she has.
2A. Have, talked
2B. No, they haven't.
3A. Has, made
3B. Yes, she has.
4A. Have, written
4B. Yes, they have.
5A. Has, done
5B. No, he hasn't.

Exercise 3 page 19

1. Have you ever used
2. Has your teacher ever talked
3. Have your friends ever studied
4. Have you ever written
5. Have you ever underlined
6. Have you ever gotten

Exercise 4 page 19

1. Melissa hasn't ever forgotten to study for a test. She has lost her textbook.
2. Franco has had trouble concentrating on his homework. He hasn't ever done the wrong homework.
3. Rose has read the newspaper in English. She hasn't ever tried to speak English with her neighbors.
4. Andy hasn't ever asked his teacher for extra help. He has been late for class.

Lesson D: Reading

Exercise 1 page 20

1. The reading is about strategies for learning new words.
2. *1.* Keep a vocabulary notebook.
   2. Make vocabulary cards.
   3. Use new words in conversations every day.
3. Make vocabulary cards

Exercise 2 page 21

1. b 2. d 3. a 4. b

Exercise 3 page 21

1. c 2. d 3. e 4. a 5. b

Exercise 4 page 21

1. strategies   4. practice
2. set   5. clues
3. plan   6. gestures

Lesson E: Writing

Exercise 1 page 22

Listening strategies: Listen to the radio, watch movies in English, watch the news in English
Speaking strategies: Ask questions in class every day, talk to people at work in English, use new words in everyday conversation
Reading strategies: Look up new words in a dictionary, read

newspapers in English, underline new words with colored pens

Exercise 2 page 22

1. Omar's first strategy for improving his reading is to read newspapers or magazines in English. He is going to read a newspaper article in English every day.
2. Omar's second strategy for improving his reading is to use colored pens to underline new words. He is going to use a yellow pen for new and difficult words.
3. Omar's third strategy is to use his dictionary more often. He is going to choose five words he doesn't know each day and check their meanings.

Exercise 3 page 23

2, 3, 4, 1

Exercise 4 page 23

Answer may vary. Possible answer:

I have learned some useful strategies for learning new words. One strategy is to guess the meaning of new words. I can look at the pictures and sentences around a new word and figure out the meaning. A second strategy is to use one new word every day. I can write the new word in a sentence and send it in an e-mail to a friend. A third strategy is to make a vocabulary notebook. I can make vocabulary cards and look at them on the bus. Another strategy is to review new words after class. I can write three new words in my notebook every day. These strategies will help me speak, read, and write English better.

Lesson F: Another view

Exercise 1 page 24

1. Read
2. Skim
3. Answer
4. spend
5. worry
6. Make
7. look

Exercise 2 page 24

1. 4
2. 5
3. 6
4. 7
5. 2
6. 3
7. 1

Exercise 3 page 25

1. 2 2. 1 3. 5 4. 4 5. 3

Exercise 4 page 25

1. 7 2. 6 3. 1 4. 3 5. 2 6. 4

Unit 3: Friends and family

Lesson A: Get ready

Exercise 1 page 26

1. came over
2. favor
3. broken
4. borrow
5. noisy
6. complain

Exercise 2 page 26

1. a 2. b 3. d 4. a

Exercise 3 page 27

1. borrow
2. noisy
3. appreciates
4. owe
5. complained
6. noise
7. favor
8. come over

Exercise 4 page 27

1. lent
2. borrowed
3. borrowed
4. lent
5. lent
6. borrowed

Exercise 5 page 27

1. lend
2. lend
3. borrow
4. borrow
5. borrow
6. lend

Lesson B: *Because* and *because of*

Exercise 1 page 28

1. c 2. a 3. e 4. b 5. d

Exercise 2 page 28

1. because
2. because
3. because of
4. because of
5. because of
6. because

Exercise 3 page 28

1. We couldn't sleep because of the noise.
2. We couldn't play soccer because of the rain.
3. They were late for the appointment because of the traffic.
4. Reyna stayed at home because of the flu.
5. Sam stayed up late because of the basketball game.
6. Beatriz moved to this country because of her children.

Exercise 4 page 28

1. because
2. because
3. because of
4. because of
5. because

Exercise 3 page 29

1. because it was closed
2. because of the rain
3. because it was her son's birthday
4. because of the smoke
5. because he was sick
6. because there were so many people

Lesson C: *Enough* and *Too*

Exercise 1 page 30

1. hot
2. tall
3. small
4. strong
5. close
6. young

Exercise 2 page 30

1. hot
2. tall
3. strong
4. small
5. young
6. close

Exercise 3 page 30

1. too young
2. old enough
3. too weak
4. strong enough
5. too small
7. big enough

Exercise 4 page 31

1A. too noisy
1B. not quiet enough
2A. too expensive
2B. not cheap enough
3A. too small
3B. not big enough
4A. too difficult
4B. not easy enough
5A. too boring
5B. not interesting enough
6A. too young
6B. not old enough

Exercise 5 page 31

1. big enough
2. tall enough
3. old enough
4. too high
5. strong enough
6. too young
7. experienced enough
8. too expensive
9. too weak

Lesson D: Reading

Exercise 1 page 32

1. The writer gets together with her neighbors once a month.
2. Some teenagers painted the graffiti.

3. My neighbors shouted at the teenagers, and they ran away.
4. The writer's neighborhood is safe.

Exercise 2 page 33

1. c   2. a   3. b   4. d

Exercise 3 page 33

1. get into
2. get together
3. watch out for
4. goes off
5. run away
6. break into

Exercise 4 page 33

1. run away
2. watch out for
3. get together
4. goes off
5. get into
6. break into

Lesson E: Writing

Exercise 1 page 34

1. today's date
2. problem
3. request
4. signature

Exercise 2 page 34

1. F   3. F   5. T   7. F
2. F   4. T   6. T   8. T

Exercise 3 page 35

1. soon
2. because
3. too
4. advance
5. Because of

Exercise 4 page 35

Answer may vary. Possible answer:
[today's date]

Prestige Apartments
286 10th Street
Burlington, VT 05401

To Whom It May Concern:

My name is [your name]. I live at [your address]. I am writing because my window is broken. Because of the broken window, my apartment is very cold. It is too cold for me to sleep in the apartment.

Could you please send a repair person as soon as possible?

Thank you in advance for fixing the problem.

Sincerely,
[your name]

Lesson F: Another view

Exercise 1 page 36

1. a   3. c   5. b
2. c   4. b   6. b

Exercise 2 page 37

1. B   3. C   5. A
2. D   4. E   6. F

Exercise 3 page 37

1. young
2. experienced
3. old
4. strong
5. far

Unit 4: Health

Lesson A: Get ready

Exercise 1 page 38

1. diet
2. exercise
3. pressure
4. gained
5. weight
6. advice

Exercise 2 page 38

1. a   3. a   5. b
2. b   4. b   6. b

Exercise 3 page 39

Healthy activities: check your weight, eat breakfast, eat fish, ride a bicycle, take a walk every day
Unhealthy activities: drink a lot of soda, eat a lot of hamburgers, eat cookies, gain 20 pounds, go to bed late

Exercise 4 page 39

1. diet
2. medication
3. weight
4. exercise
5. advice
6. health
7. tired

Lesson B: Present perfect

Exercise 1 page 40

1. have gained
2. have given
3. have not eaten
4. have started
5. have exercised
6. has gone
7. have not been

Exercise 2 page 40

1. You haven't exercised this week.
2. Paul has gained weight recently.

3. Ray and Louisa have lost weight recently.
4. Alicia has been unhappy lately.
5. My blood pressure has gone up recently.
6. Greg hasn't visited a dentist recently.
7. Sarah has given up desserts this month.

Exercise 3 page 41

1. Annette hasn't checked her blood pressure recently.
2. Annette has gone to the gym recently.
3. Annette has eaten more fruits and vegetables recently.
4. Annette has slept eight hours a day recently.
5. Annette hasn't taken vitamins recently.

Exercise 4 page 41

1A. Has Bill lost weight recently?
1B. he hasn't.
2A. Have Tina and Mario given up desserts recently?
2B. they have.
3A. Have you checked your blood pressure lately?
3B. I haven't.
4A. Has Barbara slept much lately?
4B. she has.
5A. Has Lisa started taking vitamins recently?
5B. she hasn't.

Lesson C: *Used to*

Exercise 1 page 42

1. use
2. used
3. used
4. use
5. used
6. use

Exercise 2 page 42

1. used to
2. use to
3. used to
4. used to
5. use to
6. used to

Exercise 3 page 43

1. used to eat
2. eats
3. takes
4. used to exercise
5. goes
6. used to drive
7. rides

8. used to drink
9. drinks
10. used to feel
11. has

Exercise 4 page 43

1. Emilia used to stay up until 2:00 a.m., but now she goes to bed at 10:00 p.m.
2. Emilia used to eat meat every day, but now she eats fish twice a week.
3. Emilia used to go straight home after work, but now she goes to the gym three times a week.
4. Emilia used to eat a lot of fatty foods, but now she eats salad and vegetables.
5. Emilia used to skip breakfast, but now she eats fruit and yogurt for breakfast.

Exercise 5 page 43

1A. Did Emilia use to stay up until 2:00 a.m.?
1B. Yes, she did.
2A. Did Emilia use to eat meat every day?
2B. Yes, she did.
3A. Did Emilia use to go the gym three times a week?
3B. No, she didn't.

Lesson D: Reading

Exercise 1 page 44

1. Mint is good for treating indigestion.
2. Lavender is good for treating headaches.
3. Mint is good for treating stomachaches.
4. Thyme tea can help treat a cough or a sore throat.

Exercise 2 page 45

Thyme: Use it to make tea. Use it to cook chicken and fish. Use it to treat a cough and sore throat.
Lavender: Use it to make tea. Use it to cook meat. Use it to treat headaches and high blood pressure.
Mint: Use it to make tea. Use it to cook meat and fish. Use it to treat indigestion and upset stomachs.

Exercise 3 page 45

1. digestion   4. herbal
2. treatment   5. digest
3. prevent   6. treat

Exercise 4 page 45

1. adjective   5. verb
2. noun   6. verb
3. verb or noun   7. noun
4. noun

Lesson E: Writing

Exercise 1 page 46

1. cooking and medicine
2. green-gray leaves and purple flowers
3. sore throats and breathing problems
4. to add flavor to meat and vegetables
5. as a mouthwash

Exercise 2 page 46

1. Rosemary
2. garden or in your home
3. sharp, narrow leaves
4. headaches
5. add flavor to meat or oil

Exercise 3 page 47

1. in hot, dry places
2. long, spiky leaves with juice inside
3. burns, insect bites, and dry skin
4. skin creams and lotions, shampoos, and soaps

Exercise 4 page 47

Answer may vary. Possible answer:

People have used aloe vera for thousands of years. It grows in hot, dry places. It has long, spiky leaves, and the leaves have juice inside them. You can use aloe vera to treat burns, insect bites, and dry skin. Many skin creams and lotions, shampoos, and soaps have aloe vera in them. Aloe vera is a useful plant.

Lesson F: Another view

Exercise 1 page 48

1. b   2. d   3. d   4. c

Exercise 2 page 48

1. b   2. d   3. c   4. a

Exercise 3 page 49

Healthy activities: ~~watching too much TV~~, ~~staying up late~~
Plants: ~~cholesterol~~, ~~arthritis~~
Unhealthy activities: ~~not exercising enough~~, ~~eating sweets between meals~~, ~~skipping breakfast~~

Unit 5: Around town

Lesson A: Get ready

Exercise 1 page 50

1. B   2. D   3. C   4. A

Exercise 2 page 50

1. events   4. admission
2. concerts   5. storytelling
3. afford   6. exhibits

Exercise 3 page 51

1. d   2. c   3. d   4. b   5. b   6. c

Lesson B: Verbs + infinitives

Exercise 1 page 52

1. to go   4. to eat
2. to see   5. to take a taxi
3. to meet   6. to come home

Exercise 2 page 52

1. want to ride
2. plans to eat
3. intends to meet
4. need to take
5. she expects to be
6. would like to buy
7. hopes to find

Exercise 3 page 53

1. Tony promises to visit his family every year.
2. Lee expects to finish work early tonight.
3. I plan to go to Florida this winter.
4. Shin intends to buy some concert tickets tomorrow.
5. We hope to visit our daughter in California next month.
6. Paul refuses to go to the beach this weekend.
7. I want to meet my friends on my birthday.
8. I would like to take a trip with my family next year.

Exercise 4 page 53

1. Chris plans to watch less TV.
2. Chris intends to go to an art museum.
3. Chris wants to visit relatives more often.
4. Chris plans to walk to work every day.
5. Chris would like to give up desserts.
6. Chris hopes to buy organic vegetables.

Lesson C: Present perfect

Exercise 1 page 54

1. seen   4. paid
2. made   5. bought
3. read   6. done

Exercise 2 page 54

1. hasn't started yet
2. has already closed
3. has already ended
4. hasn't opened yet

Exercise 3 page 55

1. Has, brought / Yes, he has.
2. Has, invited / Yes, she has.
3. Has, gotten / No, he hasn't.
4. Has, baked / No, she hasn't
5. Has, bought / Yes, he has.
6. Have, set up / No, they haven't.
7. Have, put up / Yes, they have.

Exercise 4 page 55

1. We haven't gone to the park yet.
2. Our favorite TV show hasn't started yet.
3. Have you bought tickets for the fund-raiser yet?
4. They haven't eaten lunch yet.
5. Ivan and Alex have already been to that restaurant.
6. Has Julie visited the art exhibit yet?

Lesson D: Reading

Exercise 1 page 56

1. F   4. T   7. T
2. F   5. F   8. F
3. F   6. T   9. F

Exercise 2 page 57

1. c   2. d   3. b   4. d   5. b

Exercise 3 page 57

1. We missed the concert.
2. The concert was superb.
3. There was a crowd.
4. The volume of the music was excessive.
5. There were five musicians.
6. The stage was unremarkable.

Lesson E: Writing

Exercise 1 page 58

Positive: amazing, fabulous, incredible, superb
Negative: excessive, irritating, ominous, unremarkable

Exercise 2 page 58

Positive adjectives: fabulous, incredible, amazing
Negative adjectives: terrible, irritating, noisy

Exercise 3 page 59

1. b, N   4. c, P
2. a, N   5. d, N
3. e, N

Exercise 4 page 59

Answer may vary. Possible answer:
Hi Ralph,
I went to the Jazz Harmony concert last week. The concert started on time, and we had fabulous seats. The band played for a long time and played some awesome new songs. But the music wasn't loud enough! The concert hall was too big, and it was hard to hear. The tickets were also expensive, and I got home very late. Maybe the next show will be in a different hall, and you can come, too.
Miss you!
Bill

Lesson F: Another view

Exercise 1 page 60

1. a   2. c   3. d   4. c   5. b   6. d

Exercise 2 page 61

1. museum   4. park
2. park   5. library
3. gardens   6. gym

Exercise 3 page 61

Park only: ride a bike, play baseball, play the guitar, go jogging, eat ice cream, have lunch, socialize, take a walk
Park and library: see a movie, meet friends, listen to music, play cards, read magazines, study
Library only: borrow a book, be alone

Unit 6: Time

Lesson A: Get ready

Exercise 1 page 62

1. to-do list   4. due
2. procrastinating   5. prioritize
3. chores   6. impatient

Exercise 2 page 62

1. a   2. b   3. b   4. c   5. b   6. a

Exercise 3 page 63

5, 3, 4, 2, 1

Exercise 4 page 63

1. chores   5. procrastinating
2. deadline   6. prioritize
3. due   7. impatient
4. tasks

Exercise 5 page 63

1. b   2. e   3. d   4. c   5. a

Lesson B: Dependent clauses

Exercise 1 page 64

1. b   2. e   3. a   4. f   5. c   6. d

Exercise 2 page 64

1. When Parvana has a lot of homework, she makes a to-do list of her tasks.
2. When she wants to concentrate, she goes to the library.
3. She doesn't let people interrupt her when she needs to concentrate.
4. When she finishes each task, she checks it off her to-do list.
5. She takes a short break when she feels tired.
6. When she doesn't hand in her homework on time, her teacher is upset.
7. She eats a snack when she feels hungry.

8. When she needs to focus she doesn't answer the phone.

9. She does the difficult tasks first when she has a lot of work to do.

10. When she has a deadline, she doesn't procrastinate.

Exercise 3 page 65

1. When I finish my homework, I take a break.
2. no comma
3. no comma
4. When we don't hand in our homework, our teacher is very upset.
5. When I have a deadline, I stay up late.
6. no comma

Exercise 4 page 65

1A. What do you do when you finish a difficult task?
1B. I rest.
2A. What do you do when you need to concentrate?
2B. I go to the library.
3A. What do you do when you don't understand the homework?
3B. I ask my teacher.
4A. What do you do when you have a quiz or a test?
4B. I study my notes.
5A. What do you do when you feel tired?
5B. I rest.
6A. What do you do when you have a deadline?
6B. I procrastinate.

Lesson C: Dependent clauses

Exercise 1 page 66

1. after he wakes up
2. after he gets dressed
3. after he eats breakfast
4. after he works out
5. after he takes a shower

Exercise 2 page 66

1. Mannie gets home before he eats dinner.
2. Mannie eats dinner before he does homework.
3. Mannie does homework before he watches TV.
4. Mannie watches TV before he reads a book.

Exercise 3 page 67

1A. What does Mannie do before he eats breakfast?
1B. He gets dressed.
2A. What does Mannie do before he works out?
2B. He eats breakfast.
3A. What does Mannie do before he goes to work?
3B. He takes a shower.
4A. What does Mannie do after he gets home?
4B. He eats dinner.
5A. What does Mannie do after he watches TV?
5B. He reads a book.
6A. What does Mannie do after he reads a book?
6B. He goes to sleep.

Exercise 4 page 67

1. I watch TV after I have dinner.
2. Before Sandy goes to work, she buys a newspaper.
3. Ivana goes to school after she finishes work.
4. After Simon finishes his homework, he takes a break.
5. They usually go swimming after they go to the park.
6. Before you go out, you need to take out the trash.
7. Melanie puts on makeup after she takes a shower.
8. Alan washes the dishes before he goes to bed.

Lesson D: Reading

Exercise 1 page 68

1. c   2. a   3. b   4. d

Exercise 2 page 69

1. impolite
2. impatient
3. punctuality
4. irresponsible
5. uncommon

Exercise 3 page 69

1. It is uncommon to miss a plane.
2. It is impolite to be late.
3. It is unusual to be early for a party.
4. He is impatient.

5. They are irresponsible.
6. She is disorganized.

Exercise 4 page 69

1. lucky
2. possible
3. honest
4. friendly
5. kind
6. rational

Lesson E: Writing

Exercise 1 page 70

1. Nita is a very organized person.
2. She keeps all her class notes in one binder with different sections.
3. She writes all her homework assignments and due dates in a special notebook.
4. In summary

Exercise 2 page 70

1. She writes all her homework assignments and due dates in a special notebook.
2. She keeps all her notes in one binder with different sections.
3. She checks her bag carefully and makes sure she has all the books she needs.
4. She plans how much time she will need for each assignment.
5. She takes a short break.

Exercise 3 page 71

My boss Frida is a very impatient person. For example, she often gets angry when you are three minutes late. She is also not a good listener, and she often interrupts. Finally, she is always in a hurry and never has enough time. In conclusion, Frida is a very impatient person, and it is difficult to work for her.

Exercise 4 page 71

Answer may vary. Possible answer:

Paula is an amazing friend. She is a very patient person. For example, she doesn't get angry when you are late. She is also a good listener. She doesn't interrupt when you are talking. In summary, it is great to have a friend like Paula.

Lesson F: Another view

Exercise 1 page 72

1. c 2. d 3. c 4. b 5. a

Exercise 2 page 73

1. waste time
2. save time
3. in time
4. on time
5. take your time
6. spend time

Exercise 3 page 73

1. Carla   4. Benita
2. Hiroshi   5. Adela
3. Paco   6. Phil

Unit 7: Shopping

Lesson A: Get ready

Exercise 1 page 74

1. d 2. d 3. c 4. b

Exercise 2 page 75

1. afford   4. cost
2. on credit   5. balance
3. cash   6. used

Exercise 3 page 75

1. $2,500.00
2. $250.00
3. $500.00

Lesson B: Modals

Exercise 1 page 76

1. b 3. d 5. c
2. e 4. f 6. a

Exercise 2 page 76

1. buy   4. talk
2. taking   5. apply
3. use   6. looking

Exercise 3 page 76

1. should   4. should
2. could   5. could
3. should   6. should

Exercise 4 page 77

1. take them back to the store
2. ask the store to send a repair person
3. buying a book about computers
4. put some in the freezer
5. sell it
6. asking her want she wants

Exercise 5 page 77

1. should we do
2. should I tell
3. should I buy
4. should I make
5. should I wear

Lesson C: Gerunds

Exercise 1 page 78

1. applying   7. losing
2. being   8. making
3. buying   9. opening
4. finding   10. paying
5. getting   11. studying
6. lending   12. waiting

Exercise 2 page 78

1. waiting   4. opening
2. buying   5. studying
3. applying   6. getting

Exercise 3 page 79

1. about   4. about
2. about   5. for
3. of

Exercise 4 page 79

1. about finding a job
2. for driving me to work
3. about getting a scholarship
4. of getting up early
5. of losing their jobs
6. in learning about computers

Exercise 5 page 79

1. Ron is excited about going to college.
2. Miguel is afraid of losing his job.
3. Vincent and Anna are happy about paying off their loan.
4. Tim and Betsy are worried about getting into debt.
5. Steve is interested in buying a new car.
6. Isabella is tired of getting home late every day.

Lesson D: Reading

Exercise 1 page 80

1. They can't afford the minimum payments.
2. They offer a 10-15 percent discount.
3. You won't have to pay any interest.

4. They say you should have at least two cards.

Exercise 2 page 81

1. Choose credit cards with low interest rates.
2. Keep the account balance low.
3. Always try to pay more than just the minimum payment.
4. Have no more than six cards.

Exercise 3 page 81

1. e 2. a 3. d 4. c 5. b

Exercise 4 page 81

1. credit   4. minimum
2. interest   5. counselor
3. budget

Exercise 5 page 81

1. interest rate
2. family budget
3. credit card
4. debt counselor
5. minimum payment

Lesson E: Writing

Exercise 1 page 82

1. c 2. d 3. b 4. a

Exercise 2 page 82

1. Gas is very expensive.
   His car uses a lot of gas.
   He needs to see an auto mechanic for repairs.
   He is worried about having his car break down.
2. Ask a co-worker to give you a ride to work and share the cost of gas.
   Drive to work three times a week and take the bus twice a week.
   Take the bus for a couple of months and save money.

Exercise 4 page 83

Answer may vary. Possible answer:
Dear Clothes Crazy,
I have a few suggestions for you.
First, pay all your bills before you go back to the mall. Second, after you pay your bills, you could cancel your store credit card. Always pay cash. Third, why don't you make a list of clothes you really need before you go

shopping? Finally, how about going shopping with a friend? Ask you friend's advice before you buy anything.

I hope this advice is helpful!

Money Guy

Lesson F: Another view

Exercise 1 page 84

1. a 3. b 5. a
2. c 4. b 6. d

Exercise 2 page 85

1. Klara 4. Luis
2. Anya 5. Jerry
3. Luis 6. Klara

Exercise 3 page 85

Across	Down
1. cash	2. account
5. interest	3. debt
6. thrift	4. credit

Unit 8: Work

Lesson A: Get ready

Exercise 1 page 86

1. employed 5. degree
2. strengths 6. personnel
3. gets along 7. shift
4. college

Exercise 2 page 86

1. reservations clerk
2. Senegal
3. cashier
4. computer, copy machine, and fax machine
5. responsible and friendly

Exercise 3 page 87

1. I'm from Senegal.
2. Yes, I am.
3. I'm a cashier in a drugstore.
4. I can use a computer, a copy machine, and a fax machine.
5. I speak French fluently and English very well.
6. Yes, I am going to college to get a degree in hotel management.
7. I am responsible and friendly.
8. No, because I take business classes at night.

Exercise 4 page 87

1. get along 5. strengths
2. degree 6. interview
3. employed 7. shift
4. personnel 8. background

Lesson B: Present perfect continuous

Exercise 1 page 88

for: a long time, one hour, three months, two weeks
since: September, Tuesday, 2:00 p.m., 2005
all: day, morning, week, year

Exercise 2 page 88

1. Kendra has been working in the library since October.
2. Frank and Marta have been studying computers for two years.
3. Carla has been looking for jobs since January.
4. I have been waiting for an interview since 1:30 p.m.
5. You have been talking on the phone for one hour.
6. We have been using the library computers all morning.
7. Kemal has been driving a cab for 20 years.
8. Gloria has been cooking food all day.

Exercise 3 page 89

1A. How long have Alicia and Claire been painting the house?
1B. Since 11:00 a.m.
For 30 minutes.
2A. How long has Inez been cooking?
2B. Since 4:00 p.m.
For two hours.
3A. How long have Tony and Leon been studying computers?
3B. Since June 1st.
For one month.
4A. How long has Yoshi been working in the hotel?
4B. Since Tuesday.
For five days.
5A. How long have you been using a computer?
5B. Since August.
For three months.

6A. How long has Lenka been driving this morning?
6B. Since 10:00 a.m.
For three hours.
7A. How long has Juan been attending this school?
7B. Since January.
For three weeks.

Lesson C: Phrasal verbs

Exercise 1 page 90

1. back 4. up
2. out 5. away
3. down

Exercise 2 page 90

1. He needs to turn it down.
2. She is cleaning it up.
3. She is throwing them away.
4. They are putting them away.
5. I need to call him back.
6. You should turn it off.

Exercise 3 page 90

1. them away 4. it up
2. it up 5. it out
3. him back

Exercise 4 page 91

1. I don't have time to call *him* back.
2. Please throw *it* out.
3. Please put them *away*.
4. Let's turn *it* on.

Exercise 5 page 91

1. She's putting away her clothes.
   She's putting her clothes away.
   She's putting them away.
2. He's handing out the tests.
   He's handing the tests out.
   He's handing them out.
3. She's cleaning up her kitchen
   She's cleaning her kitchen up.
   She's cleaning it up.
4. He's calling back Doctor Kim.
   He's calling Doctor Kim back.
   He's calling him back.

Lesson D: Reading

Exercise 1 page 92

1. Ivan wrote the blog.
2. The blog is about Ivan's new job.
3. Ivan has been writing the blog for five days.
4. He asks readers to share tips about starting a new job with him.

Exercise 2 page 93

5, 2, 4, 1, 6, 3

Exercise 3 page 93

1. c 2. d 3. e 4. b 5. a

Exercise 4 page 93

1. a 2. b 3. a 4. b 5. b 6. b

Exercise 5 page 93

1. confidence   4. patience
2. excitement   5. depression
3. fairness

Lesson E: Writing

Exercise 1 page 94

264 West Street, Apt. 41A
Minneapolis, MN 55404
August 15, 2009

Ms. Ann Robinson
Office Manager
City Office Services
2321 Central Avenue
Minneapolis, MN 55409

Dear Ms. Robinson:

I would like to thank you for the job interview I had with you on August 14th. I appreciate the time you spent with me. Thank you for showing me around the office and the supply room.

Thank you again for your time. I hope to hear from you soon.

Sincerely,

Sarah Bonarelli

Exercise 2 page 95

Answer may vary. Possible answer:
13 New Street
Houston, TX 77297
December 18, 2009

Mr. Alan Barlow
Personnel Manager
Superstar Electric Company
465 Main Avenue
Houston, TX 77028

Dear Mr. Barlow:

I would like to thank you for the job interview I had with you on December 18th. I appreciate the time you spent with me. Thank you for telling me about the training program and for

giving me the employee handbook to read. It helped me learn more about the company.

Sincerely,

Tony Wilson

Lesson F: Another view

Exercise 1 page 96

1. b 2. b 3. c 4. c 5. a 6. c

Exercise 2 page 97

1. b 2. f 3. a 4. c 5. d 6. e

Exercise 3 page 97

1. research   4. current
2. network   5. employed
3. strengths   6. interviewer

Exercise 4 page 97

1. down   4. out
2. up   5. off
3. away

Unit 9: Daily living

Lesson A: Get ready

Exercise 1 page 98

1. broke into   4. robbed
2. stole   5. crime
3. robber

Exercise 2 page 98

1. b 2. d 3. b 4. d

Exercise 3 page 99

1. crime   4. robber
2. stole   5. mess
3. robbed

Exercise 4 page 99

1. A robber broke into her house.
2. The robber got in through a broken window in the bathroom.
3. The robber stole a TV, a DVD player, and a computer.
4. Pilar's neighbor called the police.
5. Pilar should fix her window and always keep the front door locked.

Lesson B: Past continuous

Exercise 1 page 100

1. was eating
2. was babysitting

3. were visiting
4. were cleaning
5. was reading

Exercise 2 page 100

1. was knitting, was watching
2. was studying, was talking
3. was sleeping, was driving

Exercise 3 page 101

1. No, she wasn't.
2. Yes, they were.
3. Yes, they were.
4. No, he wasn't.

Exercise 4 page 101

1A. What was Anna doing at 9:00 a.m.?
1B. She was eating breakfast.
2A. What was Fareed doing at 2:00 p.m.?
2B. He was reading a book.
3A. What was Pete doing at 9:00 a.m.?
3B. He was painting the bedroom.
4A. What were Anna and Pete doing at 2:00 p.m.?
4B. They were studying English.

Lesson C: Past continuous and simple past

Exercise 1 page 102

1. We were jogging in the park when it started to rain.
2. I ran out of gas while I was driving to work.
3. Seema was having lunch with a friend when someone stole her car.
4. When the fire started, I was making cookies in the kitchen.
5. While the neighbors were attending a meeting, someone called the police.
6. Fatima was talking on the phone when her husband came home.

Exercise 2 page 102

1. was working   4. was driving
2. heard   5. hit
3. were talking 6. fell

Exercise 3 page 103

1. While we were eating lunch, the lights went out.
2. Ellen was sleeping when the fire alarm went off in her home.

3. When we got a parking ticket, we were shopping at the mall.
4. While Francisco was jogging, it started to rain.
5. While I was cooking dinner, my husband attended a meeting.
6. Julio and Tia were working in the garden when Julio fell of the ladder.

Exercise 4 page 103

1. While Chang was watching TV, the fire alarm went off.
2. When the lights went out, we were visiting out neighbors.
3. I was baking a cake when the earthquake started.
4. We were eating dinner when a thief stole my purse.
5. It began to rain while Fernando and Luis were painting the house.
6. We were cleaning the house when our daughter fell out of bed.
7. While Maria was taking a grammar test, Yan did her homework.
8. We ran out of gas while we were driving to Boston.

Lesson D: Reading

Exercise 1 page 104

1. d 2. c 3. b 4. d

Exercise 2 page 105

1. in 2006. A year later
1B. In 2007.
2. in August. Two months later
2B. In October.
3. In July, For the next three months
3B. In October.
4. At 6:00 p.m., Four minutes later
4B. At 6:04 p.m.

Exercise 3 page 105

1. b, a   3. a, b   5. b, a
2. b, a   4. a, b

Lesson E: Writing

Exercise 1 page 106

1. The story is about a car accident.
2. The accident happened one evening last week.

3. The accident happened in the writer's neighborhood.
4. He was driving home from work.
5. A cat ran across the street, the writer turned the car, and then he hit a fire hydrant.
6. The writer told his wife he was going to be late.

Exercise 2 page 107

1. b   5. b
2. a   6. a
3. a   7. b
4. b

Exercise 3 page 107

Answer may vary. Possible answer:

One evening at 5:55 p.m., Joe was sitting on a train. He was reading a book and had a box next to him. While he was getting off the train, he saw a friend and forgot about the box. When the train doors closed, he remembered his box. It was too late! The doors closed, and he lost his box.

Lesson F: Another view

Exercise 1 page 108

1. a   2. d   3. c   4. c   5. b

Exercise 2 page 109

1. e   2. a   3. d   4. c   5. b

Exercise 3 page 109

1. first-aid kit
2. emergency exit
3. smoke alarm
4. fire extinguisher
5. neighborhood watch

Exercise 4 page 109

1. d (smoke alarm)
2. a (fire extinguisher)
3. b (first aid kit)
4. c (emergency exit)

Unit 10: Leisure

Lesson A: Get ready

Exercise 1 page 110

1. c   2. d   3. e   4. a   5. b

Exercise 2 page 110

1. days off   4. books
2. discounts   5. tax
3. round-trip   6. reserve

Exercise 3 page 110

By plane: $85.00, $269.00, $354.00

By train: $234.00, $134.50, $368.50

It is cheaper for Fabiola to travel by plane.

Exercise 4 page 111

1. Room rates are high in the summer.
2. Summer is the most popular season for tourists.
3. You can get a discount if you book ahead.
4. You can reserve your hotel room online.
5. Sam has three days off.

Exercise 5 page 111

1.
$300.00
$300.00
$38.00
Total: $638.00

2.
$500.00
$360.00
$39.00
Total: $899.00
Money they will have: $51.00

Lesson B: Dependent clauses

Exercise 1 page 112

1. get, will go
2. will travel, aren't
3. is, will ride
4. visits, will stay
5. don't, won't

Exercise 2 page 112

1. If Jack's friends come over this afternoon, they'll play soccer.
2. If the weather is good, the Perez family will go hiking.
3. If Stacey has the day off, she will go shopping.
4. If it rains this weekend, Robert will read a book.

Exercise 3 page 113

1. have   5. comes
2. will visit   6. will go
3. will you do   7. doesn't come
4. don't have   8. will visit

Exercise 4 page 113

1A. What will Brian do if he has time off this summer?
1B. He will go swimming.
2A. What will Tam and Chen do if the weather is beautiful this weekend?
2B. They will work in the garden.
3A. What will Sara do if she gets some extra money for her birthday?
3B. She will go shopping.
4A. What will you do if you have a three-day weekend?
4B. I will go hiking.
5A. What will we do if the weather is bad?
5B. We will clean the house.
6A. What will Anna do if she finds a cheap flight?
6B. She will fly to Seattle.

Lesson C: Dependent clauses

Exercise 1 page 114

1. leaves	7. leaves
2. goes	8. leaves
3. will read	9. will buy
4. reads	10. will get
5. will find	11. will put
6. will choose	

Exercise 2 page 114

1. Before Victor books a flight to Dallas, he will talk to a travel agent.
2. Victor will make a hotel reservation before he flies to Dallas.
3. After Victor cleans up the house, he will leave for the airport.
4. Victor will go through security after he checks in.
5. Before Victor returns from his trip, he will buy presents for his family.

Exercise 3 page 115

1. a. Pedro will buy concert tickets before he invites Nick to the concert.
   b. Pedro will invite Nick to the concert after he buys concert tickets.

2. a. He will invite Nick to the concert before he makes dinner reservations.
   b. He will make dinner reservations after he invites Nick to the concert.
3. a. He will meet Nick after he finishes work.
   b. He will finish work before he meets Nick.
4. a. He will go to the concert after he eats dinner at a restaurant.
   b. He will eat dinner at a restaurant before he goes to the concert.

Exercise 4 page 115

1. What will you do before you go on your trip?
2. What will Trina do before she goes on vacation?
3. Where will they go after they leave New York?
4. What will Suzanna buy before she reads the newspaper?
5. Where will Danh and Giang go after they cook dinner?

Lesson D: Reading

Exercise 1 page 116

1. T	3. T	5. F	7. T
2. T	4. F	6. F	8. F

Exercise 2 page 117

1. The Statue of Liberty is the main topic of this article.
2. It's located in the middle of New York Harbor.
3. France gave the Statue of Liberty to the United States.
4. They gave it as a gift of friendship.
5. It's the day of America's independence from Britain.
6. There are 354 steps inside the statue.
7. You could see New York Harbor from the crown.
8. If you want to visit the museum, you need a Time Pass.

Exercise 3 page 117

1. a	3. b	5. b	7. b
2. a	4. a	6. a	8. a

Lesson E: Writing

Exercise 1 page 118

Answers may vary.
Possible answers:

1. Central Park is a popular attraction because it offers something for everyone.
2. a. There is a zoo, where children can touch animals such as goats and sheep.
   b. There is a beginner climbing course with indoor and outdoor climbing walls.
   c. There are row boats on the lake.
   d. There are concerts and theater performances.
3. If you feel tired at the end of the day, you can take a ride around Central Park in a horse-drawn carriage.

Exercise 2 page 119

Answer may vary. Possible answer:

One of the most popular tourist attractions in California is Hollywood. Hollywood has something for everyone. If you like movies, you can visit the movie studios. You can also see the footprints of movie stars or walk along the Hollywood Walk of Fame. If you like music, you can go to a concert at the Hollywood Bowl. Hollywood is a fun place for people of all ages to visit.

Lesson F: Another view

Exercise 1 page 120

1. c 2. b 3. d 4. b 5. a 6. c

Exercise 2 page 121

1. Yosemite National Park
2. Paris
3. Paris
4. Waikiki Beach, Hawaii
5. Sebastien and Eve